PROBLEMS OF THE WORLD
Reality Check

by

Derrick D. Brown

RoseDog Books
PITTSBURGH, PENNSYLVANIA 15222

The contents of this work including, but not limited to, the accuracy of events, people, and places depicted; opinions expressed; permission to use previously published materials included; and any advice given or actions advocated are solely the responsibility of the author, who assumes all liability for said work and indemnifies the publisher against any claims stemming from publication of the work.

All Rights Reserved
Copyright © 2006 by Derrick D. Brown
No part of this book may be reproduced or transmitted in any form or by any means, electronic or mechanical, including photocopying, recording, or by any information storage and retrieval system without permission in writing from the author.

ISBN # 0-8059-9905-1
Printed in the United States of America

First Printing

For additional information or to order additional books, please write:
RoseDog Publishing
701 Smithfield Street
Third Floor
Pittsburgh, Pennsylvania 15222
U.S.A.
1-800-834-1803
Or visit our web site and on-line bookstore at
www.rosedogbookstore.com

I have spent my life trying to make the right decision for every situation that came into my life. The decisions that I have made, made me who I am today, like any other human being. I have also made the wrong decisions and I have paid for them but I also learned from them. I also feel like God has us all here for a reason, even if it is to just try to make a better life for our children and to find our souls and also to find our way to heaven. I also feel that I have found my way and I want this book to teach children how hard life really is, and to see how life can bring you satisfaction mentally, physically and emotionally. I want the world to know that you can get out of poverty through spiritual decisions of the mind and the soul, because when you make the wrong decisions you know it in your heart as well as in your mind, and I also want my 7 children and other peoples children to survive the devils traps of life.

This book is based on my life and all the things that people should know and why it is important to know about who is running your life and who is running the world and how they are running it, also, the things that people should have been told, but were never told, such as: the Masonic orders of the world and where your money is going and why things in life seem so hard and even things you should know about your government and the world around you. This book will also teach you the mental control of your everyday life, the symbols and signs that you might see in movies, on churches, in hospitals, and even on your money, and you will never pay any attention to them, also you will find out that the Masonic control of the world and the secrets that you never knew how important in your life it really is, and also you will find out there are parts in your history that were written about but never talked about, such as: Adolph Hitler Masonic order/Knights of Malta secret society, the Pope's Knights of Malta secret society, the Queen's crown was the Masonic square/Knights of Malta, British rites & Scottish rites, the royal family, George Washington's chair where he signed all of his documents, school and college rings, Chrysler symbols, Shell gas station/dawn of a new day secret society & the problems of the world. So America, wake up and make this book not a reality check but a reality change, so the world's children can see a future again.

Special Thanks To:
NBC, ABC, CBS, CNN, MSNBC, The History Channel, & Fox News for all my resources and information on Politics.

Santa Clause Article By: Alauddin Shabazz

Bush Picture: Time Magazine

Other Pictures: Free Times

Arnold Shwarzenegger & Hitler Picture: LaRouch Article.

Reason for the Book: For America could wake up and see the light.

Author: Derrick Brown

Written By: Venus Whitmore-Brown

And last but not least, thanks to all of my sources on all of my information and the Masonic information: internet, tapes, movies and books.

Contents

Chapter 1: My Life Story 1-19

Chapter 2: How You Can Change Your Life and the Lives of Your Children 19-20

Chapter 3: How Your Life Is Controlled 20

Chapter 4: Crime 20-21

Chapter 5: The $ Bill & Sign/Symbols 21-68

Chapter 6: Problems of the World 69-137

This is my life story back as far as I can remember.

I was born in Birmingham, Alabama at Jefferson County Hospital. My Aunt Jean told me that at the age of 1, I was really sick; I had a fever of about 200 degrees as I was told, I was on my death bed not even old enough to live a life yet. The fever would not break so my mother and my grandmother rushed me to the hospital, which is when they told my family that it was yellow jaundice. When I was in the hospital they put me in a tub of nothing but ice so that my fever could break, they told me I was in a coma for about a month before my fever even broke, and I was told my body was so hard that you could beat me in the chest with a sledge hammer and I would not have felt it. My fever finally broke about a month later, and I was all better then. There was another time I had a near death experience when I was about 6 or 7 years of age, me and my brother Vincent was playing in the backyard of my grandmother's house and we were throwing rocks at the pecan tree in my grandmother's backyard, we would climb on the roof of the house and we would throw rocks up at the tree, then we would come down and get more rocks to throw at the tree so that the pecans would fall. So one time I picked up a brick and took it up on the roof with me and I went to throw it and I didn't let go in time and it slung me with it and I fell off the roof and cut my knee on a piece of metal that was buried under the ground. I had about forty stitches in it and my knee cap was on the side of my leg, so they sewed it up and put a brace on it and sent me home. I went home and I feel asleep and my mother came in to make me go to the bathroom, she was trying to wake me up, but I could hear her but I couldn't get up, it felt like someone was holding me down, so my brothers Mark and Vincent came in and they picked me up out of the bed and took me to the Jefferson County Hospital and they told my family that I had blood poisoning and rust had got up into my blood stream and they had to put me in a bubble. They put a tube in my neck to help me breathe and they put one in my stomach to feed me. I stayed in the hospital for about 6 months.

There was this pretty nurse that was so nice to me, she would bring me some McDonalds and my grandfather brought me a television from the house because there was no television in the room where I was. My grandfather got mad because they would not let him in the room to plug the television set up for me; they told him that he had to look at me through the glass. My family told me I was in a coma for a long time and that is some messed up stuff. I remember one day I was at my grandmother house riding the big wheel trying to do wheelies and I feel in a ditch by the car line and broke 2 of my toes. One day me and my brother was going through the woods in the back of my grandmothers house, we saw panties and shoes and other stuff and then we found out by watching the news, there was this guy called the cape man killing people and one day I seen him at the Piggly Wiggly Grocery Store when I was with my grandmother and he had on this long trench coat and he had a knife chasing people. We pulled up in the store then we seen that he was chasing people, so we turned the car around and shot right back out of the parking lot. I thought it was just a myth until I seen it for myself. One day I remember my mother and my aunt was fighting and I forgot what started the fight, but every time my mother would get paid she would buy everyone something to eat and my aunt would too, but one day my aunt came and got her kids and took them to get something to eat and left us there and we were hungry. My mother and my aunt started fussing about the matter and they fought for a long time and the thought in my head was; I wish this would just hurry up and be all over and done with. Another bad experience was when my grandmother came in the house fussing with my mother, they came in the house and grabbed a knife and went back outside and got back in the car and left to go find this lady my grandfather was messing with, my grandmother had just seen them together, so the lady and my mother got into it and my mother cut her up with the knife so bad, that when she went to court they told us that we had to either leave town or she was going to go to jail, and that is when we moved to Cleveland. My Uncle Ray had already moved up here and he already had a job and my Aunt Jean had already moved up here too, and she had a job. When we moved up here we moved on a street called Orville and the school was right across the street from our house. My brother Vincent had a friend and his friend's mother told us that she used to do voodoo, and she used to have these little voodoo things all around the house, she used to say she can put curses on people and make their hair fall out and have all kinds of bad luck. I used to believe her because she looked like she knew that type of stuff. My brother Vincent had another friend that owned Tees Pet Store on 105 and Superior, and he still owns it to this day. My brother Mark had a friend that he used to hang with and was his best friend, one day my brother Mark wasn't around and Mark's best friend was picking with my other brother Vincent, and I guess he thought Vincent wasn't going to fight him back because he was older and bigger than us, and he pushed my brother Vincent and my brother Vincent pushed him back, and then he swung at Vincent and Vincent said the dude hit him in the face and Vincent rushed him and the dude fell backwards on the ground with my brother Vincent on top of him, and they was swinging on each other and Vincent caught his hand and bit a plug in the dude arm, and later on that day we saw Mark, Mark was mad that Vincent bit the dude but Mark asked Vincent did he want him to beat him up again for him and so Vincent told him no, I beat him up enough. The house we stayed in had a lot of rats. I was lying in the bed and I felt something in the bed with me and I thought it was a rat and it was the spring in my bed. I remember when we got our first be-be guns, we would walk down by the woods go across the bridge on St. Clair, and one Christmas we had these red carpets that my mother had bought us, and we would ride them down the hill, and I remember this kid that lived on our street was with us and he didn't have no magic carpet, he had a sled. He rode the sled down the hill, and when he did he got stuck up under the fence, because he couldn't stop at the bottom of the hill. The bottom of the fence was stuck in his chest and they had to come and pry him from under the fence. We used to do a lot of stuff to have fun. But I never thought that once you get grown and move on your own, it would be so tough. I didn't think I would be able to make it without selling drugs, but things was so tough because everybody know that everybody was doing the same thing at the same time, and that was selling drugs. I didn't really know anything about where drugs came from until years later and that it would have such a big impact on life, and I didn't know it was going to change my life. I think that it changed a lot of people's lives. And I think people didn't know it was our politicians and higher authorities that helped them to bring it over here. A lot of things you don't expect, the politicians controlled by the decisions they make. Some things you have to work hard to get, but some people can just go and get whatever they want and whenever they need it and some people can't. It took me a long time to know that in life sometimes you have to struggle and strive for what you want. We was staying on Linwood after we moved off of Orville, and we got some bikes for Christmas and we used to ride them in the basement because it was freezing cold outside. Me and my brother Vincent use to make weights with old paint buckets and put cement in them and put a broomstick in the middle of them until they dried up, and that is where we lived when we learned Gymnastics. There was this man that knew how to flip and asked us if we wanted to learn and I remember one day I was flipping and I got messed up, my legs missed the ground and went through, I went to high and I landed on my back. Two months later my uncle Michael moved up here and he had a goldish color car, but I can't remember what kind it was, and I remember my mother took the car and went to the bar and on her way back home from the bar and she said somebody was trailing her, so she put the car in reverse and backed into the car that was trailing her, and when she came in the house we went back out to the car and the rear of the car was bashed in. We called the police and reported it stolen after we parked it up the street, and they called us to come and get the car and my Uncle Michael was very mad about the car. When we were kids, my uncles Clemen, Terry and Michael thought they were the best basketball players ever. There are a lot of things that can change what you do and how you think about your life. Some things that change me were after we moved from Linwood, we knew how to flip, and we were real good. We moved to 30th projects, it was like everything was different; it was always somebody to play with. It was a store across the street and I hated going to the store with food stamps like most kids, and I would pay somebody to go in there for me, because if they caught you going in the store with food stamps, the other kids would talk about you for days. It was like if you took a dump in school and the other kids found out, they would talk about you until graduation. I remember when I first got my virgin hood broke. Me and Vincent, it was always me and Vincent. It was these 2 girls from the old projects. Vincent went in the room with one girl and I went in the room with the other girl. She took my pants down and rubbed it until it got hard the way she wanted it and then she took my pants off and hers too and then she stuck it in and it felt funny like I wanted to take it out but I didn't. It was like a tingly feeling, and that was the only time I messed with her and I never spoke to her again. I was about 12 years old when it happened. I had a friend name Philip and he was from Trinidad and he knew how to draw real good. It used to be this big head white dude and he knew how to draw real good too. We were making art pictures for this contest and I won first prize, but the 2 dudes could draw better than me, and the picture that I drew is still in Merling Sterling Elementary School to this day. It is a picture of all different races holding hands, playing basketball, and all kinds of stuff. It was the idea that I came up with that made me win first prize. I remember when I used to come from school and my brother Vincent was a crossing guard and I used to run pass and hit him in the stomach and run to the house. Me and Vincent made the basketball team, baseball team, at the Bath House and the coach Bud came up with a flipping team after we taught other kids how to flip in the projects. We went up to Glenville for tournaments with the Teen Titans and went to other tournaments and we would win them, and then we started break dancing and formed a group. One day we was break dancing downtown and this man wanted us to break dance for a birthday party for Councilman Ed Flynn, and one of the men that was downtown was the man from M.A.S.H., it was the first time I ever seen somebody from TV, close up anyway, the councilman paid us 25dollars a piece for doing the show for his birthday party. My mother bought us some suits to do the show in. Bud, our coach used to pop us in the head and Bud used to call Mark lead feet, and say, boy you got lead in your ass, you going to slow. Bud was our basketball coach and he was also like a father figure and kept us out of trouble. I remember as we got older, we used start going down to the Rascal House, and right next door there another bar called Bollies. We used to put a iron clothes hangar in the Ms Pac Man game and put a whole lot of credits on the game, and we used to get a quarter and put a hole in it and put a string through it and put it in the Dig Dug game and keep snatching it out and putting more and more credits on that game. My brother Vincent had a friend named Melvin that used to take us down to the Rascal House and buy us pizza, because he had a job as a kid. Although they stayed cracking jokes on each other, they still were best friends. I remember when we first moved down to the projects on 30th, the 30th kids tried to jump me, it was about 8 of them and I thought I knew karate so I was kicking and they ran like hell , like this dude is crazy. And I remember one day, I was about 14 years old and this girl I was talking to on the phone and she told me to come over her house and knock on the back door because her father is sleep, and once he goes upstairs he won't come back down, and so me and Vincent went over there and knocked on the door and guess who answers the door, her father, and he asked us what we wanted and my brother Vincent asked for a girl that I know, and he said the girl he asked for didn't live there and before we knew it he turned to get a shotgun and started shooting at us and we ran like hell and the next day I seen the girl and I told her that she don't have to worry about me calling her never ever never ever never ever again. And as I got older and started working at Sunoco, I seen her and her father and her father didn't even know who I was but she did, and I still didn't say anything to her, because she tried to get me and brother killed. I remember my mother boyfriend used to walk to work in the blistering cold just to take care of us. I remember one time they got into it and my mother walked to go get my brother Mark from this lady house and my stepfather was right behind her and she told Mark that they had been fussing and Mark beat him up, and Mark wasn't nothing but a 16 years old then. One time my stepfather was cheating with this woman and my mother came home fussing and she poured hot water on him and burned the mess out of him. He woke up screaming loud and me, Mark and Vincent ran in the room and we thought our mother was going to go to jail because of how bad it looked and leave us, and we were scared, but he did not call the police. I remember when I was 14 years old, I met this white girl downtown when we were break dancing, she liked the way I was dancing and we talked on the phone a couple of times, and we hooked up downtown and we had sex downtown by the statues over by the stadium and we didn't know it was people there until we stood up and then we ran. There was this place called the Eagles Nest, it is located on 55th between Cedar and Central, it was a place for 18 under age kids to go and party. My friends and I used to go up there all the time and all of our other friends from 30th would already be there, but this time wasn't anybody from 30th there but my friends and I, so some of the dudes from other projects seen that we were the only ones from 30th that was there, and they decided to try and jump us after the party was over. This girl that I went to school with that was at the party told me to watch my back, and just so happen I snuck my knife in the club inside of my boot, because they search everybody at the door, the party was over and we were walking out and all the dudes from the other projects were standing outside waiting on us to walk through them and when we got half way through them, one of the dudes said something to Richard and Richard turned around and the dude swung on Richard, so we turned around and said wasn't anybody jumping in it, and that is when a dude swung on me and Vincent caught him and hit him and all of them rushed us, that is when I fell backwards and I grabbed my knife and I jumped up and stabbed the first person that swung on me and after I stabbed him, his friends grabbed him and ran with him and then the rest of them rushed us and I went and started swinging the knife until I got to my brother Vincent and then I told Vincent to run, so we all ran except Anthony, because he was already gone after they swung on his brother Richard. We ran all the way from 55th to 30th all the way to the house. So later that day the police came down to the house and ask for the knife, by that time I cleaned off the knife and threw it away. Then I had to go to court for assault, I had to keep going back and forth to court, but nothing happened. Before I got sentenced my mother went to the hospital and told us to clean up the house, we were waiting for her to come back home and she never did. So my family came in and sat us down and told us that our mother passed away at the hospital. We were all crying and my brother Vincent stood up and started throwing things around. That night when we went to sleep the house felt so empty. It still is the worse day of my life. My brother Mark moved in with my aunt and we moved to Alabama with my grandmother. I was hurting for a long time; it was like somebody pulled out my heart. In Alabama our grandfather would get us up early in the morning to eat breakfast, because in Alabama you got up early in the morning to eat breakfast. On the weekends he used to take us to work with him. Isn't it funny how history repeats itself, I ended up having to move to Alabama for the same reason I had to move to Cleveland, my mother got into it with somebody and it went too far. But life holds a lot of consequences and repercussions. I started going to Jones Valley High School and my uncle was already going there and he was known to be a gang member, when I got there I was labeled the same thing, the teachers treated me different from the other kids. The teachers seemed prejudice in Alabama, we used to go over to the skating rink and sometimes we would be walking back, and some white dudes will be throwing whole cans of beer at us, but they did not ever hit us with anything. I was still in school at the time my uncle Terry started drinking and then I started drinking while I was still in school. We used to go down to this bar called Tees Place and we wasn't even old enough to be in a bar, we went to Tees Place to pick up chicks and try to get some ass, because that is all that was in there. Sometime I would get so drunk I would not even be able to get up and go to school the next morning. My grandmother knew that we were drinking because one time Vincent threw up all over the floor, the wall and all on his bed. There was this girl I met in the bar and she had a gold teeth in her mouth and she used to work at Stanford University, I moved in with her and she got me a job at the University. I started loosing my family because I would never go and see them because of this girl. There was this dude named Barry that used to work with us. He had a girlfriend and she used to cheat on him. One day he picked her up and pulled over to the side of the road in between 2 cemeteries and told her if I can't have you then nobody will, she thought he was about to do something to her but he shot himself in the head. The next day I heard about it at work and it was so quiet at work. Then I moved back with my grandmother and everybody was missing me then. They used to tell me "boy you don't never come and see us no more!" And I told them, "I don't have a car". So my brother Mark drove up there and he bought me a car. When he came up there he had a Mohawk in his head. Not too long after that they had to leave back out, and everybody was sad saying goodbye, it was a very sad time saying goodbye. Uncle Terry started working out there with my grandfather so he could save enough money to buy him a car. He saved up enough money and he bought him a car for 100 dollars, and the dude he bought it from told him the water pump was broke, after he got the water pump fixed the car would not start, the motor was messed up and it was sitting on the side of my grandmother's house. We went to the junkyard and stole some radios to put in the car and one day one of the wires from the radio touched and blew the radio, so we went to go get some more radios. One day we went and got some radios from up by the school and there was this van and we got in the van and Terry couldn't get the radio out so he started tearing the whole thing out, the dashboard and everything. Then a whole group of people came running around the corner and a girl Terry knew was with them and she told on us, so we ran and they chased us and we drop the radios, we ran through the ditch and jumped the fence, we ran down the railroad tracks and through the ditch, the water was cold, it was winter time. Not too long after that, I went to school and they called me to the office and the police was there and this man was in there with them. The man told us that sometimes he sleeps in the van, because he takes medication and we were lucky he was not in there or he would have shot us. The police asked us why we did it, and we told him to buy me some shoes, because I needed some shoes. My brother Mark used to send us money so we could buy shoes and stuff. Lavertha is the girl that I moved with and she had an ex-husband and he sold cocaine, and he used to come by and drop the kids off some money and some toys. Lavertha worked at Days Inn and she got me and my brother Vincent a job there with her. Then I started talking to the manager and I started drinking too much and they laid me off, but Vincent was still working there. While I would be at my grandmother house, Lavertha would be at the house with her ex-husband messing around and I didn't know how to handle that. So I went and got my clothes from her house and moved back with my grandmother and that made me stronger. Vincent started talking to the barmaid at the bar and her name was Sandra, he got her pregnant and they used to all types of things together like go to the movies and stuff like that. It was like I couldn't keep a woman because I could not stop messing around on them with other women. I figured if you want me, you are going to have to want me for who I am and not who I mess with. You are going to have to want me for my heart and not what I am doing out in the streets. It is like you mess around 2 or 3 times, you don't know where it comes from, then after that you both start messing around on each other, and that will lead to somebody getting hurt, and who knows you might be crazy enough to stab somebody. Then I met this girl name Tammy. My brother Mark came and got us and took us back to Cleveland and I was still calling Tammy. My brother Mark was talking to this girl name Marguerette and she had a twin name Marguree, and I started talking to her and she kept my mine off Tammy. My brother Mark took care of everybody when he was selling drugs. One day Mark came in the house and said this dude done got me robbed, so we didn't have no money to eat or nothing, so his friend loaned him some money to get back on his feet. Around that time we were going back and forth to court about my mother and we were going to get a lawsuit settled, and we won the case. We put all the money in my Uncle Ray's name, and we bought us all some cars. We took care of our families. When you are born you are paying bills. Not too long after that, we bought cars and we treated people the way you suppose to treat people. One day the police came in and busted the house, they took everything with them and we had to start selling cars and selling things so we could pay bills. Mark let his friend use his car and he got pulled over and they arrested him and took him to jail and they towed the car. Mark went to try and get his friend out of jail and they arrested him on a secret indictment and Johnny and Dice got arrested too on a drug case. So we moved with Mark's girlfriend Tammy and she moved with her mother. So I did what I had to do to pay the bills and my cousin Ernestine moved in with us. I started talking to a girl name Regina and I was supposed to have got her pregnant but I found out it was not mine, it was this other dudes that she was messing around with. One day I kicked in his door and she was in the room and he ran down to the basement and went and got his gun so I left.

I was hurting bad because I was living with her and she did that to me. My cousin Ernestine used to take my girl, Regina to this other dude house. One day we went to the movies and after we left the show, my cousin Ernestine had on a dress and you can see what color panties she had on, and this dude was like, oh I see what color panties you got on and my cousin Ernestine was like f you and the dude said f you b, so they was back and forth fussing with each other, and at the time she was talking to a friend of ours named Black Terry, he came over there and the dude was big as I don't know what, I came over there and the dude started talking mess and so I said, man we about to leave, I guess the dude thought I was a hoe because he swung on me, and when he swung on me, I caught him and I beat his ass. So everybody took their coats off and threw them in the middle of the street. We beating his ass and Ernestine start beating his girl ass and Terry beat his dude ass. So the police was pulling in by that time and we done went and got in the car about to pull off and the dude told the police we stole his coat, but black Terry picked up all the coats and picked up his by mistake. So they charged us with strong armed robbery, we was out in Maple Heights at the $1.50 show with all of our kids. One day I called myself selling drugs to pay bills and the vice was rolling, so I was like I'm about to go on the blossom so I can get out of the way, and this is when the Malcolm X hats came out and the shirts and somebody just robbed Mr. Hero on 74th with the same thing I had on, the dude that robbed Mr. Hero ran in the bar and went to the bathroom and took off his shirt and hat, I was on the dance floor dancing so the police came in and snatched me off the floor and took me in Mr. Hero and the lady was like it was not me, and so the policeman Eugene was like check him anyway because he is one of the dope boys, so they check my pockets and I didn't even get a chance to take the stuff out of my pockets and I called myself getting out of the way of the police and ended up getting caught anyway; that is how funny destination is anyway, because when it is going to happen it is going to happen anyway. When I went to jail my so-called cousins robbed me and stole my rent money. After that I got out and went to court and they got the whole story and everything that happen and everything that took place, after they transferred the files downtown for us to go to court downtown, they dropped mine down, and they dropped my cousin down and my brother never went to jail because he didn't fight and Terry pleaded guilty to it because he had other charges, so they dropped the other charges so he could plead guilty to that, and he did like 8 years, and they dropped Ernestine charges and she never even went to court and she was the reason the whole thing started. Everybody came to court and told what happen, so we paid a fine.

So a year went pass and me and my brother Vincent, were up in the California Club, we walked pass this dude, and he stuck his hand out for Vincent to shake it, so my brother shook his hand with his other hand because he had a drink in other hand and the dude say I ain't no b***h, and my brother was like, Derrick this dude talking stuff because I shook his hand with the other hand, and I was like f that n***a just keep on walking, and the n***a like dude and we turn around, and the n***a done pepper sprayed me and Vincent, I can't see nothing, all of a sudden I hear the n***a say get em, so I see him and grab him and get to whooping his ass, and Vincent get to whooping his dude ass, and the dude was like all right we cool, we quit. So the dude left out and grabbed a meat cleaver out of the kitchen and was hiding behind the door, and I grab a knife and Vincent walked out first and it was crowded and Vincent couldn't hear me saying watch out watch your back, and the dude hit Vincent in the head with the meat cleaver and I stuck the dude in his side and tried to rip him all the way up with the knife, we stopped this car and they rushed Vincent to the hospital and I went to this girl named Nee-Nee house that I met 2 weeks prior to that, because I was too scared to go to my house. So after that they was looking for me, and the detective that was on the case couldn't find a lot about the situation, because the dude didn't want to press charges and Vincent didn't want to press charges either, because Vincent didn't want the dude to send me to jail, so the dude got out the hospital and wherever we were we always watched our back a little bit more after that because that was one experience that I swear to God, I wished I could have stopped what happened; but there are some things that you just can't stop, because destiny is a bitch but it also teaches you things too. I knew not to trust nobody then, not even the people that you are friends with.

After that, my brother Mark was still in jail doing 13 years, and we in the streets still trying to make it, charges never came up on me because didn't nobody want to press charges. So I stayed with the girl Nee-Nee and we were having problems because I couldn't stop being with other women, and I was serious about my life but I still had kicking it on my mind. Not too long after that we get into it, so me and my cousin Ernestine planned on getting a place together. I left Nee-Nee alone because she got to telling my probation officer that I was always out kicking it and everything. At the time I'm still working for Abe at the gas station on 55th and Cedar. That is a good man, he help me raise my family, him and my brother. I think without him or my family, I don't think I would have made it, and I don't think I would have made it without my brother Vincent and his moral support, not this far, because I used to think about crazy stuff. I think back on how I used to think and I believe I changed for the better.

My cousin Ernestine mother Jean went to jail, she had shot my cousin Earnestness abusive baby father. He killed the cat, and he used to get into it with my brother Mark and Ernestine would get mad at my brother Mark for helping her. One day we was at the bar and Earnestness abusive baby father jumped on Ernestine and somebody called my aunt and she came up to the bar and Ernestine and Annette came out of the bar and he started throwing bottles at all of them then he rushed across the street with a bottle in his hand and my aunt Jean shot him and she went to jail for 11 years. Ernestine and her siblings were on their own and so was my and my brother Vincent. My grandfather came to Cleveland for the trial. When I got ready to leave this girl named Nee-Nee, she kept all my clothes, radio, and my identification. When I went to go get my clothes, she called the police and told them that I was threatening her; the police came over there telling me that I had to get out of there, so I left with no clothes. I went over to my job and got an early advance on my paycheck to buy me some clothes. After that, I was working and I thought I would not be able to make it without selling drugs and working, but working is slow money but it is worth it and you don't have to worry about getting your door kicked in or nothing of that sort.

Now things are different, a war has started, hatred is everywhere, hatred of priest, hatred of people in general and it is like everybody just hates their lives or everybody act like they hate their life and half of them act like they want you to kill them.

——My brother Mark was still in jail, me and Vincent was struggling trying to send him some money, he thought it was alot of money out here until he got out of jail and he seen that life is a struggle now, it is not like back in the days when was then called ballers, we used to throw parties, cabarets. Mark went to jail at one of the parties we threw for white Jesse, the police showed and tried to jump on everybody, they hit Mark in the head and Mark fell to his knees, and this lady cop tried to grab his balls, they was talking about they are some dope boys and this a dope boy party, then they grab me and throw me to the ground, the police hit Vincent in the back of the head with a shotgun and threw him to the ground. About 30 people went to jail that night.

I remember one time we were up at the park, and Alan was on the other side of the park, and this dude was like you don't remember me and swung on Alan and the rest of the dudes jumped in and started whopping Alan's ass; from the top of the hill to the bottom of the hill, and so Kissie said they are jumping on Alan, so everybody started to run to the bottom of the hill and started swinging on everybody that was jumping Alan, Johnny arm flew out of socket when he hit a dude and so I ran up and swung on the dude and knocked him to the ground. After that we ran back up the hill; leaving the dudes in the middle of the street knocked out, so we got into our cars and pulled off, as we were on our way to the house we saw the police going into the park to see what was going on, and later that day the police rode pass the house that we were all at and rode pass and kept on going.

People act like material things really matter, but they really don't. I am on probation now and working hard and not thinking about selling drugs and my brother Mark is in jail, and I worked hard all the way up until I got off papers which was 8 or 9 years later. My brother realized how hard it was out here and he became a hard worker although he has always been a hard worker, and I am proud of him. I am proud of my brother Vincent, he has 3 beautiful kids, and all of us do. Life is funny now I'm older and my body aches sometimes; my back hurts, but I'm still working hard.

One of my bad baby mama experiences was with Regina, who told me all through her pregnancy that the baby was mine and even though I knew she cheated on me, I was still with her through her whole pregnancy. She had the baby and she found it wasn't mine, so she wanted the baby's real father to come around who she cheated on me with and also used to be a friend of mine, so we just started slowly moving apart from each other and she started spending time with him, so I stopped messing with her, and then she met some other dude and left her baby father alone, but after a year she kept trying to come back to me, I guess she couldn't take it without me, she kept trying to come back for a long time. She had everything, the dude she was with gave her anything she wanted, such as cars, houses and credit cards and even a motorcycle, money just couldn't satisfy her. Money doesn't satisfy anybody. While I was in jail, which is when she started cheating on me with him while we were living together, after I got out she kept on cheating on me with him. She used to tell me it was her girlfriend's dude because she was always is in the front seat. She would have him coming to pick her up and her friend would be in the car like it is her friend's man, but they would drop her friend off at the bar and they would go to the hotel. My other baby mama name is Bridgette, she let my brother Mark girlfriend Lafonda talk her into talking to some dude that stayed around the corner from my brother baby mama house, I was looking for her and I couldn't find her and my brother baby mama called me and told me where she was and set her up, so I go over there and beep the horn and she came on the porch and I told her to get in and we started fighting and I took her over my house and we broke up, I took her to the house and we was back and forth messing around until we just stopped, by that time she was pregnant and I stuck with her all through the pregnancy and she had the baby name Derrick, while she was having the baby she went into a seizure because she couldn't take the pain, they kicked me out the room and gave her a c-section and took the baby out of her. My other supposed to had been baby mama name was Shaun. When we had a lot of money she used to act like she was so in love, and I always knew she was crazy but I didn't know she was crazy enough to do what she did to me. I heard about her at the hotel with a friend of mine name Meech, so I stopped talking to her and I started back talking to her, but we was just messing around, it wasn't that serious, then she got pregnant. I stopped talking to her while she was pregnant and she used to always threaten me and I didn't ever think nothing about it, so one day she got her mothers car and at the time I was talking to this other girl named Ronda that had the same kind of car I had and we was leaning on her car and looking at a fight up the street between this lady and this man and wasn't paying any attention, so Shaun came down the street and snatch the car over and hit me and I flipped up in the air and fell down and the mirror went into my leg, she went and parked the car at her mothers house around the corner on 79th, my brother Mark pick me up and put me in the car and took me to the hospital because my leg was wide open and I got about 60 or 70 stitches in my leg and my knee was messed up, you could see all the way through my leg to the bone. I got out the hospital the next day and I went home, by that time the police had picked her up and took her to jail and I talked to my family and they talk to me and the only reason I didn't press charges on her was because she was pregnant and I didn't want her to have my baby in jail, so I dropped the charges and about 6 years later she called herself being mad because I didn't have no more money to be giving out and she went and filed child support on me and come to find out the reason for her staying out of jail was because I thought the baby was mine, I found out the baby wasn't even mine. That is something I don't understand, you spend all your money on a child and you keep the receipts and find out that the baby isn't even yours, you can't go to court and get your money back, they will tell you it is a gift, but they will hit you with back pay if you are just now going down there. After that I was still living with Regina and I got Stacy pregnant, Shaun baby name is Deericka and Stacy baby name is Derricka. They were born a month apart. At the same time Regina was pregnant I had another Derricka on the way, but Regina's baby wasn't mine. Bridgette baby was. But I always treated Regina's baby like she was mine. I was with them for so long all she knew was me as her father. I started working at Sunoco, Abe leased it to Salty and Abe moved down to Grandpa's. So I was used to staying in one place and it was hard for me to change, so I ended up being down at Sunoco for another 2 years, while I was at Sunoco, I meet this girl named Tanya, I used to hang with this dude name Smiley, and he has a baby by Tanya. So one day I am was in the Zulu's and she was in there and she started talking to me and by the time I knew who she was, we were already messing around and she got pregnant and I got twins by her, beautiful twins, Derrin and Derrick, bad, but them my boys. Things didn't work out between us because I can't stop being a whore and she talked a lot of mess and I didn't like that. Not too long after that, this girl named Melody, started working up at Sunoco with me, she had an attitude and she had a stalker. One day she went to get her car washed and Sleep used to wash her car and a tape got stolen out of her car by somebody and she said Sleep did it, so her dude came up there and slapped Sleep, so he went and told Vincent and the other dudes and they went across the street to the gas station where the dude was, and they said her boyfriend was scared to come out of the store, because they were going to beat him up. So Melody looked at me and then looks at him and Melody said, don't think he is going to help you because those are his people. So after that he was really scared then, so the dude left and he did not ever come back up there anymore. My brother Vincent was at the car wash and my friend named Polo had got out of jail by then. Polo went to jail for being stupid and scandalous. I guess he couldn't take having no money after the dope game wasn't in anymore, and he went Donald Trump on everybody (ha,ha,ha). After that Polo stopped going to jail and Vincent stopped being at the car wash because they were trying to close it down, so Abe sold the car wash to the City Mission. After that I started dating Melody because her dude wasn't coming around anymore, and that is when she got into it with Essa and he fired her. A month later I quit and started working down at Grandpa's with Abe, my first boss. I moved in with Melody and while I was at work, she was cheating on me with the dude that used to stalk her. It hurted because I tried hard with her and I slowed my cheating ways down, but she left me with nobody to go back to. So she had a lot of bills that she had built up on her and I tried to give her the money, but she didn't accept it and she said she was going back to the dude, because he was paying all of her bills and he had bought her a new car and gave her credit cards and had a good ass job, so she went for the money, she left me because the dude had some money. And just like Melody, Regina left me for the money, but the money back fired on Regina, I hated it back fired on her, but it did though. Regina was the first person that I was with for about 4 or 5 years. After that I started working at Grandpa's and Regina used to come around and she was trying to get back with me. After that, I met my last baby mama, her name is Venus. I am still with Venus, she went through a lot at first, I was still a hoe for a long time and she knew it and she stayed by side, she cried a lot and threw tantrums a lot, but I guess she learned to put up with my different crazy ways until they changed, I stuck with her and still I am with her, we have 2 boys together, Darius and Daquawn. All my kids names start like mine and I didn't name none of my kids, my baby mamas named them, except my last 2, I named them. But it would have gone like this: Derricka, Darrika, Derricka, Domonique, Derrick, Derrin, Darius and Daquawn. I love all my babies; I would die and go to hell for them. And Venus she is a good girl but she don't know when to stop fussing sometimes and can't handle her liquor sometimes, but that is my baby and she makes me happy, she keeps my mind off of a lot of things that goes on in my life too. She is one of those people that stay happy and when you are around them they brighten you up because they are always happy, always. Things weren't always good between me and Venus. I am going to tell you about an incident that I think brought us closer together. One night we were drinking and we got to fussing and I forgot what it was all about and I took her home and it was about 2 o'clock in the morning and I dropped her off and I went home and went to bed, about 3:30 or 4:00 in the morning she came bamming on the door and hollering so I didn't let her in because I knew if I would have let her in we would have started fighting and I would have went to jail and so I called the police and they came and I told them to just take her home, they took her outside and ran her name and I didn't know she had a warrant, so they took her to jail and she kept calling her family to help her out and no one would come and get her out or help put up any money to help get her out, so I got the money and I went downtown and got her out, after I was the one who put her in there, I went to court with her and stood by her side and she got 90 days of house arrest and 3 years of probation, it was something that she did before I met her. So everything wasn't always gravy, there was ups and there was downs.

So now I am down at Grandpa's Kitchen with my old boss Abe, and he was still trying to get his land back and the Jews wanted it to put the pictures in their bible on the wall and hopefully someone would pay attention and help him get his land back. His father was a veteran and he died in the process of paying off the money for the land, but Abe's mother worked really hard and bent over backwards paying for the land and taking care of her kids, but there is some things that money can't replace, and if you break your back working, can't anything replace that, and the way this world is now everyone is taking everything for granted and everybody is starving and it is like nobody sees the homeless and they are steady making people homeless by taking jobs away and laying people off of the jobs that they already have.

So we started doing a talk show talking about political problems and things going on in the world, but it seems like I never get a chance to say what I wanted to say because the show was short, but then they gave us an extra hour. So I started writing a book on the world's problems and the decisions the Politicians made on any and everything. I wrote a paper that if anybody had anything to say about political problems or problems the politicians have caused by the decisions they have made that caused an affect on them, to write it down and send it to me at Grandpa's Kitchen, then I found out that the things that I found out, I couldn't put them in the book because the information that the people gave me was from other people, so I started to write a short story on how I got to where I am now all the way from the beginning. Now I am writing this book and I am going to put what was going to be the front cover on the other book on this book but change it a little bit. I am doing the show for free and I don't mind doing it because it gives me a chance to speak the way I feel about the politicians and their decisions they made, but I wish we was making some money off of it but hey that is how life is and I learned how to be satisfied with whatever you got when you got it and I taught myself how to be satisfied with money when you got it because it is not what you do with it when you got it, it is how you use it when you do get it, because I have had it and I lost it and a lot of it was taken away and it still gets took away with every income tax check. Child support takes it and it don't bother me none at all.

In the book it was not suppose to be like this, it was suppose to be a book on how fast life is going on and how fast time is moving and on how many people is dying, on poverty, on joblessness on education on racism, and all the bad things that is going on in the world. All this different information that you learn, and you only hear about it once because no one is allowed to write about it because it is someone else's information and I think everybody needs to know about it. All our privileges are gone, police gone, ambulances gone, and firefighters gone too, schools short, people out of jail and more and more murders are happening all over the world, there is more missing children. There is one problem that really concerns me the most is that the kids are starting to dress like adults and when I was a kid we got our clothes from different stores like Value City and JC Penny and we dressed our age and now it is really different. Now they are letting all these rapist and murderers out of jail and putting our kids in harm's way. They are taking all of these mothers off of welfare and they expect someone to be home when their kids get out of school, but yet and still they are making parents go and find jobs and get off of welfare, and they wonder why more and more kids are growing up too fast and being teenage parents, the reason is because some parents have to be out all day and all night either working or looking for a job. We all believe we are living in heaven but the way the world is we are all living in hell. I seen the movie The Passion of the Christ and I loved it and it makes you open your eyes on different things about life and how Christ gave his life for ours, and it seems like when you are living in hell the only place that seemed to be left to go is heaven, so you should make sure that you get your lives and the lives of your kids together because it is coming soon.

Now I have a place of my own, me with my uncle, but I live with a young lady name Venus and I love her and she loves me and we went through a lot together, she stuck by me through my hoeish ways and I have told her that I am grown and I will sleep with whoever I want and it is nothing you could do about it and she stuck with me and she is still sticking with me, she stuck through worser stuff than that but I am not going to tell it all because it is no one else's business. But I have 2 kids by her and I am satisfied with my life and working at Grandpa's and Abe lease it to some Indians and they are all right and that Abe is a mover. I wrote this book because I didn't want to be considered or thought about or forgotten and especially of all as a quitter, because I have never been a quitter at anything I ever did. I help as many people as I can when I can. I don't treat people any different from anybody else; I go off on people just like any other person when they piss me off. I know that I am going to heaven because I am satisfied with my life and I don't have to do anything bad, and I know when I go, I am going to be there with the politicians if they get to heaven and I believe they are going to take them last because of the problems they caused the world.

A couple things that inspired me to write the book.

First of all, I went out and registered to vote, and I found out that I can go out and register other people to vote. I held a voters registration rally at the Neighborhood Outreach Center on 85th and Madison on the 25th of September and I invited different candidates and no one showed. After that I tried a petition, I had 2 petitions that I wrote and I put the petitions in the book and I had people sign them and no one showed me how to put them forth and I still had people sign them and I had them at different store locations. I found out that it doesn't matter who you vote for because everyone is being controlled by someone else.

When I was staying with my uncle, there was this young lady Tammy that he was with that kept on pressing charges on him and getting them dropped whenever he said that he did not want to be with her anymore. One day she press charges on him that she could not say that she lied about this time because it went to court. While he was going back and forth to court I got up some evidence that was not ever used in court and sent it to the judge and I took it to the lawyer and to Fannie Lewis and she gave the judge a call to take a look at the papers, but she said that they had to come from my uncle's lawyer, so I gave them to the lawyer and he never gave them to the judge I gave him a lot more evidence to give to the judge but he never gave any of it to the judge. There were also other things that happened in the case too.

My Jail Experiences:
I never made hooch but I have drunk it, the feeling you get when they first bring you in, they strip you down, take everything that belong to you and they give you accessories like soap, toothpaste, toothbrush, they put you in the shower and spray this stuff on you that kills crabs just in case you have crabs, then they take you to your room and lock you in, it is like living in your bathroom. You get bored and tired of being there and start missing your family and your freedom, and you start feeling like your life is wasting away. Most people get out and end up right back in there again for the same thing that sent there in the first place. Jail holds a lot of experiences, most experiences in jail, none too physical, you can't go in there thinking you are bad because someone is going to jump you or they will try to jump you, so the best thing for someone that is in jail to do is to stay to themselves and do their time and watch your back and watch your locker box because people steal. Most of the fights that occur in jail were because someone stole something from somebody. But it is a waste of life, because if you had a

house when you went in you won't have it when you get back out, most of the time when you get out you won't have your girlfriend, if you have a job you won't have it when you get out, a lot of people owe payments on their cars when they go to jail, when they get out they won't have it, you loose most of your life when you go to jail, and when you get out you spend most of your time trying to get it back, but it is not possible to get back what you have lost, because time doesn't go backwards for anyone it goes forward, and the feeling that you get when you get out is like I don't want to go back there again. You spend all your time hustling when you get out to take care of your family and when you get caught, you spend all your money that you earned trying to keep yourself from going back to jail, it is like when you do something your family always have the repercussions of everything you do.

My first getting out of jail experiences:
The first one is when I was with Regina, I wasn't in there long but she thought I was going to be in there long, but since it was my first time in, I was eligible for shock parole. So after being in there for a while and I was hearing things that she was doing, I would hear about all the men she was messing with, one was suppose to been a friend of mine and when I got out she wasn't at home, when she found out that I was out she was scared to come to the house thinking I was going to do something to her because she knew I heard everything about what she was doing while I was in jail but I didn't, she was just trying to survive and I told her to survive when I was in there and to do what it takes, because she had kids to raise. I cut my hair when I got out and I was bald head, I was wearing jail house shoes and the jail house clothes. We got back together and it didn't last long because I couldn't put out of my head all the things that she did while I was in jail, so every time I would call her cell phone and she wouldn't answer it, I would think she out doing something, so we fussed until we got tired of fussing and then we wasn't together anymore.

My second jail experience, I was already on the run for a probation violation for a year and I was still up to my old tricks and I didn't know how to survive without selling drugs, so I was still up to my old things. The last time I went to jail I said I would never go again, and here I was on the run because I messed up again. I got caught on 90th, I was staying with a young lady name Nee-Nee and I was on my way to her house, right before I crossed the street to go in the house, the vice stormed the block and they grab me and grab a couple more people and I gave them my brother Vincent name, but I couldn't use my brother name because I had warrants and I knew that once we got downtown and they fingerprinted me they were going to know who I was anyway, so I told them my name and I was downtown for 3 months waiting on the trial thinking I had another case because they told me that they found something on the ground and what they found was not real, it was salt, so they dropped those charges. Shanucy Thomas Jr. was my lawyer on the case, so after talking to him and telling him what happened, and what I was on the run for, he knew it was for a probation violation, so I told the judge everything that happened and how I was living my life and all the things I was going through at the time, so he reinstated my probation and after he reinstated my probation, I had to do it all over, so I wasn't going to get off of probation until 99", so they let me go and that was the last time I went to jail.

How You Can Change Your Life and Your Kids Lives
When you are young, you never think how important life is, the only thing on your mind is getting money, getting paid, buying fancy cars, buying fancy clothes and getting all the women that you can, and you think that is the life; when you have to start paying bills and you don't have all that money and all them fancy cars or clothes, that is when you think how important life really is and how important your kids are and how to change your kids destiny so they won't end up like you were, behind bars or even dead. Then you start to find out what the law is all about and how it limits you to do certain things in life and the way you raise your kids, when you know how to raise or discipline your kids because they are yours to raise and discipline. Once your child is in the system, it seems like it never stops and it goes from juvenile to adulthood and the older you get the more harsh the crimes get, because it gets harder to get money and money is becoming more scarce, it is like they are getting us ready for the end of the world and I hope not, but it seems that way.

I used to think that all the things that I did in the past would stop me from going to heaven, I was thinking that all the bad things I did and all the women I was messing with and worshipping things instead of life and money instead of life, I thought I was going to hell until I stopped and seen everything that was going on in life and all the different things that was going on in the church's, I saw a war that was started because of terrorism that seems like it is never going to end, I see all the different people dying on the news, I see all the kidnapping going on in the world, I see all the people that I saw when I was a kid, being downgraded and drug through the dirt and ridiculed, and children have no one to look up to now and the politicians and the different decisions that they are making and the money that they are taking and put it in their own pockets, instead of helping the people that they are given the money to help. I know the dirt that I did can't never amount to the things that they did, so I know I will be going to heaven. And I know I'm going to heaven because I am satisfied with life and I don't hate anyone for anything they did to me and I don't feel no pity on no one, I don't wish no one was dead and I don't wish no harm on anyone, and I am just satisfied with me and I think that if you have hatred in your heart you won't get into heaven because God sees that dark spot on your heart, so you have to forgive everyone that has done anything to you, once you forgive people for the things that they have done to you, because it seems like there is nowhere else to go but heaven.

How Your Life is Controlled
I am going to try my best to take you through step by step on how your world is being controlled by other people right in front of your face and right in front of your eyes without you even knowing it, the good things as well as the bad things.

What would you do if you didn't have to worry about the children, their families, and they don't have to worry about crime on the street, consequently they can concentrate on who's running the government or how fair the laws are and so there for, it's better to keep people occupied, but not for a long time, that is why politics are called political science. There's a method to controlling people. It's a science. If you can see people organized or disorganized, frightened, fearful or broke; that is another thing, they want to keep you financially in a hole, then people are subservient to you and you don't want people to become self-sufficient and have enough money so that they don't have to listen to you. You need crime and you will see why you need crime and let the criminals back out on the street, they talk about something, and if you think about the logic of behind these rules and behind these laws and stuff, it is absolutely insanity. So a criminal goes out and kills somebody, what do they do, they take the gun away from the criminal and they let the criminal go free and get out on bond. Speaking of crime, it's out of control; the drug trafficking and all the killings and the gangs killing each other, but the point is if you don't pay your income tax or if you do something that is against the government and if you get out of line, they will find you; the FBI or the IRS, if you don't pay your income tax, you can go into the Amazon Jungle and they will come down there looking for you even if they have to spend 7 million bucks they are going to find you and bring you back here and make an example out of you. So they have the power, this is the most powerful military nation on the face of the earth, ever devised by men. This nation is the most powerful military combine on earth, it has always been, and if you think about the time back in **1940**, when the United States was a very infantile country, and it didn't have all of the high technology it has today, and in just a couple short years it got itself together and was able to meet on the field of battle throughout the world and was able to do a battle with the whole Nazi empire, but they can't do anything about the drugs. The problems is that they have total control over everything, so when you see things going on, just understand that the power could be in this government and they want it that way. Franklin Roosevelt publicly, most of you know who that is; Franklin Roosevelt made a statement publicly, he said, anytime you see anything happening in politics, you better understand it was planned that way, so anything that is going on in this country that sounds crazy and lunacy is crazy and lunacy to you, but to those guys that are doing it, they know what they are doing, there is a method to it. On the back of the dollar bill you will see a symbol on the left hand side of the bill, it says Annuit Coeptis, which means our enterprise is now a success or our enterprise is crowned with success. So you say fine we have an enterprise and it is crowned with success, what enterprise are you talking about? Norvus Ordo Seclorum, Norvus, which means New, Ordo is Order and Seclorum is where we get the word World, so it is New Order of the World or New World Order. George Bush's New World Order is now a success. But the problem is this was put on the dollar bill back in 1934. 1934 is when the Federal Reserve actually finally took total control of the United States monetary system and that is when they said it is now a success, because this is a symbol, this is an emblem of the secret society.

A secret society of freemason called the Illuminati is German Zebrallian Illuminati, they were a secret society salvaged in the South of Germany, called the Illuminati or the Illuminated Ones; the Enlighted Ones. They began to connect themselves to another group of freemasons from France, in the south of France, referred to as the first temple grand masons, and the symbol today on the 1 dollar bill, it is also on a document in the British museum and in the Luke museum, both have some of the original writings of that set of freemasons in Germany and on one of the documents, it has the exact symbol, Anuit Cueptus, Norvus Ordo Seclorum, and that was in 1774 that the Bavarian Illuminati drew up their plan for what they were going to do in America and how they were going to do it, so that is not anew, that is not just for 1934, that goes all the back to 1774, its a symbol of the secret society. The triangle at the top with the white illuminating from around it is horrid, the god of the ancient Egyptians, of course this is an

Egyptian pyramid and you don't find them in America, you find them in Egypt, and that pyramid is the symbol of the eye was in the Egyptians religion horrid, which was the new born son, every morning the sun came up, his name was horrid, there was the so on divinity in Egypt, horrid was god son the light of the world, who is wisdom, he is the wisdom savior. And so horrid was referred to as god's son, and that is why the light is illuminating from around because its the sun, the sun is the round eyeball of God, the ancient Egyptians believed the people of Gaza thought God was the sun watching them and therefore the sun was very bright, and so today we say someone who is intelligent is brilliant, they are bright, that is why God is the most brilliant of all, therefore the sun is the most brilliant because it is God's eye.

There are 13 layers on the pyramid and the 1776 at the bottom, most people think it is because that is when the country was founded, it has nothing to do with that, this is on a document, published back in 1774-75 and in 1776, the Roman Numerals appeared on it in Europe. So what an anions do is just the 1776 is when this secret society founded itself and put itself into operation. In the other secret society or fraternal order, near the few years in the formage of saving, and then there is time when they actually get a conquer and come together and actually become a actual organization, and they get a carker from the government, legalizing them as an organization. They ran operations in 1760, 1770, but it wasn't until 1776 that they actually made themselves into a coherent order and called the order, illuminati. They were the base of for what we call today in our country, Bavarian Illuminati is the bases for what we call the Colombian faction, the Colombian Faction of the Illuminati came here right after this government was formed and that is where we get today's Colombian movies, Colombian television, Columbia Records, Colombian University, matter of fact Columbia Broadcasting System, what is the symbol for CBS, it is the altering eye, it is the Colombian fashion of a secret society that calls themselves the Colombian, and that is why our government is in the District of Columbia, because these guys own our money and they also own our government and they also own you, you are their property. Matter of fact, when you are born and on the bottom of your birth certificate, it says the Department of Commerce, it is a property of the Department of Commerce, because you are nothing more than a piece of commerce old material. That is why when you are out of work, you don't go to the Unemployment Office, you go to the Human Resources Office, and so you are just a human resource. So in other words, these guys print the money, run the country and they own you and they own everything around it, and so they make the laws and they decide who kills who and who can get away with it, because they make the laws and they decide. So the secret society, the 13 stripes the 13 stars, which make up the Star of David, the 13 berries the 13 leaves and the 13 arrows,

everything is done in 13 because 13 is an unlucky number, the reason why we say is unlucky because, it is an divinely inspired number, it has to do with God in Heaven and therefore it is unlucky to you and it not suppose to be used by you. 13 of course is base on, this is what we call Masonic Symbolism, and freemasons divine the sale of bill. Everything is done in secrets of 13, and again I draw your attention to the 13 stars, which make up the star, David, there is a reason why. On the dollar bill, just to show you how clever these guys are, on the one dollar bill at the top of it there is a little owl, the symbol of the Bohemian Society, they meet in California on the last 2 weeks of July of every year. The Bohemian Society is a secret society that will sprout off of another secret society, the Colombians have a little fan club that they meet for 2 weeks out of the year in Northern California, they are called the Bohemian Society, they meet in something called the Bohemian Grove. All of the Presidents are at the Bohemian Grove in Northern California, and they are wearing red and black Klu Klux Klan dress type of thing with the pointed headdress and everything.

That is quite frank to see the presidents dressed up like Klu Klux Klan members and they are standing in front of a big open pit of fire and behind them is about a 20-25 foot owl behind them

and the article in the Time Magazine shows you the same picture, it says the Presidents meet with all of the heads of state in the world and all of the most wheelers and dealers in this country and they all meet up in Northern California, they have rituals where they go before the owl after midnight. All the Presidents dress up in Klu Klux Klan outfits with black and red robes on, before an owl, and the reason why they chose the owl was because it is a symbol used in Europe by secret societies because the owl is wise and it sees things in the dark. And that is why they know things you don't know, so they see things in the dark and they put their little owl on the dollar bill, it's just a clever little thing to show you how these guys think.

Getting into Masonic Symbolism, when you drive by a freemasons Masonic lodge, you will see a square and a "G" in the middle, it doesn't stand for God, it stands for Geometry, it goes back to 1717 it stood for Geometry, the "G" has been used by secret societies as far back as Ancient Greek, meaning the Genesis Principle, the principle of generations or sexual sensible. So just remember when you see that "G", remember it stands for Geometry. So talking about geometry, the square, circle and the triangle all have Masonic and spiritual meaning to them. Here we have the square within the magic circle. Incidentally the Washington Monument is amobuline, and on the dollar bill there is another Egyptian symbol.

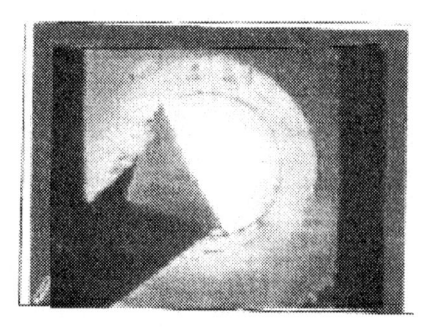

America is referred to by the secret societies throughout the world as the new Egypt. Because our whole lives is based on the magic of Egypt, the white and black magic, which is why the police have black and white cars. We have the mystic star, it is a 7-pointed star, if you see the secret societies, and you will see it all over. With the military, you see them give the thumbs up signal, that was developed for America by Alex Secrolli, one of the most master magician known over the world, he also for England the victory sign, the "V" for victory is form the Jewish Masonic symbol for benediction of life. Symbols and emblems don't just happen; they are there for a reason.

The 7-pointed star, the California Highway Patrol uses the 7-pointed star. It is a magical symbol, the 7 of course is the reason we have 7 days of the week, the 7 candle lamp stand, everything is done with 7, it is a very important number.

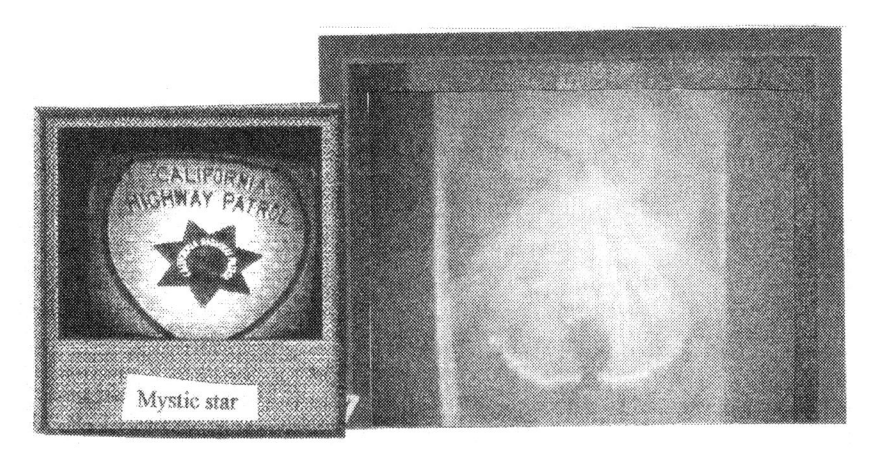

The double cross which was Roman freemasonry, the double cross which is Eastern Orthodox is used for the double cross. That is where the saying "double-cross" comes from, which means, being deceived or being cheated. On Exxon the double cross is there. Exxon said they did it that way because they are freemasons. They will tell you as long as you were to smart enough to figure it out.

The 5-pointed inverted pentagram, it is really something that represents evil. Penta of course, means 5, if you take the "r"'s off of a pentagram the star and you have just the inside, you have what is called a pentagon, which is why the United States has a pentagon. The pentagon is a symbol, that is why incidentally Chrysler uses a pentagon symbol for their Chrysler symbol because they are the ones that produced all of the tanks and everything else for the United States in the 2nd World War for the pentagon and they still use the pentagon for a symbol. Here is a picture of an upside down pentagon with the point pointing down and the 2 points sideways, and this is a symbol representing the devil and you see all of these killers and rapist with the 5-pointed pentagram tattooed on their arm or their neck.

PROBLEMS OF THE WORLD

5pointed inverted pentagram

5pointed inverted pentagram

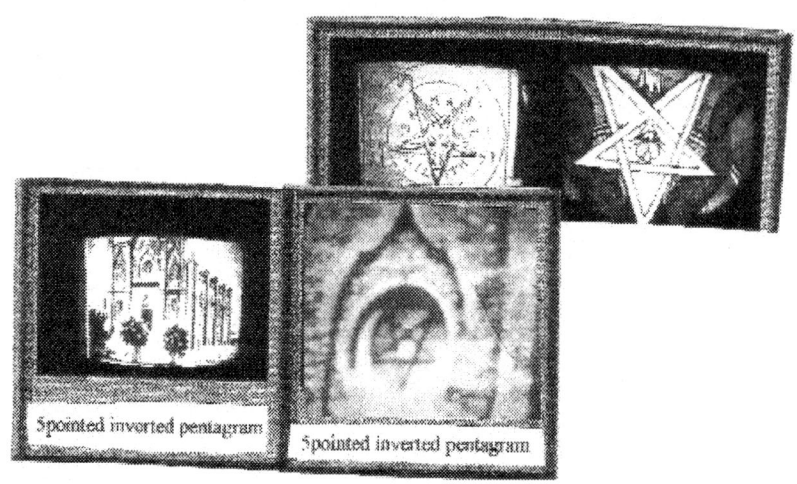

The 1st pentagon was in Los Angeles and it is an inverted pentagram and like everyone knows, it was devil worshipped in the early ages. Incidentally the 7 candle lamp standing in the pentagon represents the 7 lights of the heavens: Mercury, Venus, Mars, Jupiter, Saturn, the Sun and the Moon, the 7 ancient Gods of the ancient world, when you see the 7 candle its a very holy 7 candle lamp, say no; it is representing the 7 moonlights in the heavens. Each one of those lights represented a God and each God represented a day, which is why there are 7 days of the week, to honor the 7 candle lamp and the 7 ancient Gods of the world.

7 lights into heaven

There is a sun rising between 2 triangles, the sun rise is a secret society in Europe and it is used in a good way and they said yes, and it has been used for over 100 years since the nark of the never lands, it is a never ending secret society. There are different kinds of symbols around and we don't even know what they mean.

The reason for the devil's square, the first square means that you play fair, when you play baseball, you play down at the Town's Square and when it is right in the secret society, you play fair and square. When you go to jail, they give you 3 square meals, its fair and it's the right thing to do. So when it comes to square, it means everything is right and when you go to court, they tell you your story doesn't square with the fact, square means with the right and correct. When you super impose another square, the implications of the second square means disorder, or that you have the power over what is right and correct and you also have the power over disorder.

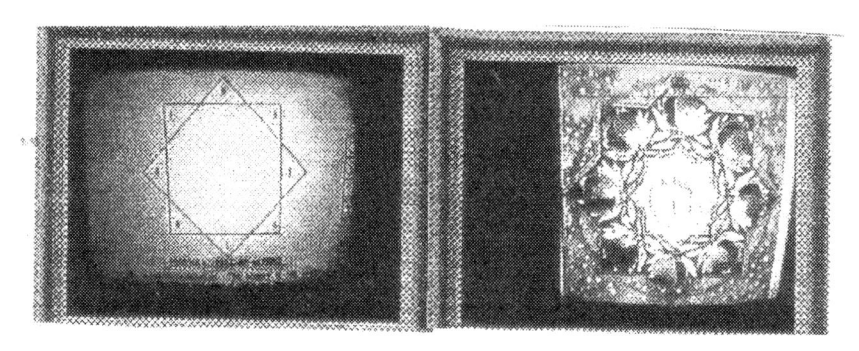

What does the Chevron stand for; Military and the police wear on their arm, they are called Chevron, it is a square, a box. The squares are sitting on top of each other of the Chevron of the double square of freemasons.

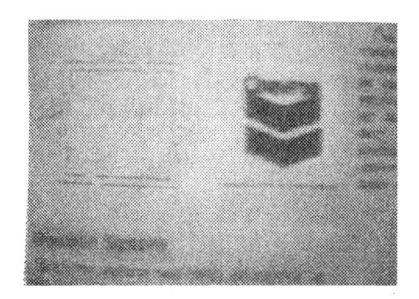

They control over power, revolution, anarchy and they have control over this government and Russia's government. It implies that they have both control over revolution, trouble, anarchy and they have control over good government. They can do whatever they want, if they want a good or bad government they will have one, they can do whatever they want, because they have the money and the power.

Here in England, of course its more appropriate in England is the double square freemasonry in London at the parliament. The octagonal library has the double square freemasonry,

of course it is appropriate there because they do in fact organize and direct all over the world, all kinds of blood shed and violence all over the world is being organized, directed and financed by the United States government and the British government together, Britain and America for the reason for violence and chaos we see in the world today, and Yugoslavia has all been planned as part of something that the United States is doing in the middle east right now and Yugoslavia is going to pay for it.

Here is the double square of freemasonry worn by the Queen.

This square is the Masonic square referred to the light of Malta square, this one is the British square freemasonry the light of Malta, you will see it is like in the form of a triangle together, but they don't actually have a point or round with nothing in the middle, you will see that again in Arco,

4 little points come together with nothing in the middle. The light of Malta is pyramid on the top looking down on pyramid of Egypt without the capstone, which is because how on the dollar bill the capstone is not connected to the body of the pyramid. So here flying over the top of the pyramid looking down on the great pyramid you don't have a point, because the cornerstone is not on the pyramid.

We hear a lot of people talking about fascism on the radio and television, but on most cases fascism has come to power after economical collapses, are we having problems economically or what? The Vietnam and some other disasters, the fascist party went mass support by promising to revive the economy and restore national pride. That is what the government is saying today, they need to restore national pride.

No one seems to realize that Bill Clinton is a rode scholar, trended England and London England and Oxford University, bought and paid for by the Rockefeller Foundation financed and organized his education, he is nothing more than a yes man for the power elites in this country, they want another Kennedy cause he looks good.

Personal liberties of severely limited under a fascist government and the government also control newspapers and radio and other means of communication. Issues of propaganda to promote its policies. A secret police force quests any resistance, you get in their way they come out and beat your brains out. Here is a symbol of fascism:

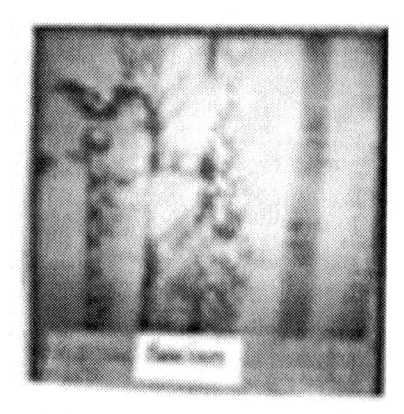

A bundle of sticks with a hatchet head, incidentally you always see the red seal.

In England, you hear the story of Robin Hood, in the movie of Robin Hood, Earl Flynn is standing behind the red seal, because the red seal is German for Roth Siles, Roth Siles of England where German Jewish families and England took over the bank of England and took over 5 other banks in Europe and became known as the Roth Sile Banking Dynasty of the World, the richest banking dynasty on earth. Roth Sile in Germany, Roth is red and Sile is flag, and everybody knew that the Roth Sile were the biggest murdering bunch of thieves and thugs the world has ever known, oh sure they were wealthy and they had banks, they were high class thugs, and so they were called "hoods," and that is where we get the term hood from, they went around the world robbing, and that is why they are called "Robin Hood." Robin Hood is the hood that was robbing people in the Sherwood Park and that is the home of the Roth sile was, this is Sherwood Park, "The Robin Hood." The red seal lifestyle and the symbol was the franchise, this is the symbol for fascism. Fascist was a political movement that developed in Italy and several other European countries in 1919, this name was derived from the ancient roman symbol of authority consisting of a bundle of rod and a ax, that is incidentally why we have an axis power in the Second World War. Here is the bundle of sticks and the ax:

This is on the back of a dime, the symbol for fascism on the back of the American dime,

and it says fascism is a dirty, evil government that takes over and controls the people, of course it does, that is what is happening to us, we are being taking over and controlled by fascist. The president giving a state of the union and standing on each side of him is a fascist, this is in the congress, in the congress the symbols of power for the president are 2 large fashise and very few people noticed them, they are looking at this guy and they don't even see this symbol are world fascist power. The idea of the bundle of sticks was in the Roman Empire, that Rome could not police the world, yet what Rome needed to do was collectivize a police force, that is why George Bush is talking about not just us in the middle east, it is a group of us, we barely represent a contusion of a group of nations there, not just America, that's the concept of fascism, it is not 1 stick it is many sticks joined together with a hatchet head, so 1 person, 1 government can't do it, Bush says. What we need is a united nation where we can all unite our sticks together and now we got power. Now everybody crawls on their knees and kiss his boots because they have a collective incentive of fascist ruling. We have a fascist rule government right here in America.

The United States Senate to fashise on the Senate, and in the playing cards you have the fashise with the King and the Jack that means something, there is a reason why the ax is the ace, but it is called something else, ace is always higher than the king for a reason.

There is another geometric symbol used in freemasonry by the secret society, it is a triangle, a pyramid within the circle again:

and incidentally the pyramid or the triangle is important because it goes back to the old pyramid of sceot, when incidentally the pyramid of sceot has no point on it, on the circle it represents the sun and it has to do with stone hinge, stone hinge is a symbol for the sun and the old ancient secret society, that is why stone hinge and the pyramid are connected and numerology and stone hinging and the pyramid are both the same, there is a lot of interesting stuff that when you get into the numerology of the pyramid and stone hinging. Here is an example of how symbols are used, you will see the cross and the crown again, the "G" that suppose to stand for God, but it stands for geometry, the triangle and circle again, it is the top of the triangle and the circle and it has to do with God, it is a symbol for God in freemasonry.

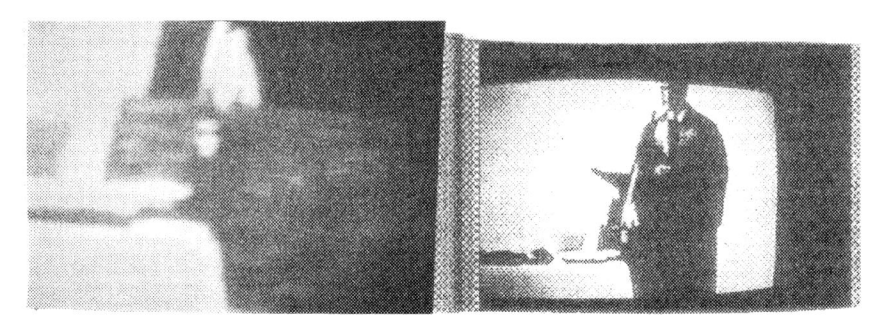

The Star of David, in freemasonry you may have heard of The Royal Arts Degree and you will see that is used in churches, the school of Theology in Claremont, because Claremont School of Theology is a Masonic College it is financed, organized and directed by a secret society in Europe and the people don't realize it because it is a holy, it is a church, this is a very powerful secret society that is operating throughout the world, behind our government and other governments around the world and they have tied themselves in and set up what they call a religious establishment and this establishment is nothing but a front man for a very powerful secret society that is operating in the world, they make look holy, but you better do your homework, there is more to this religion than meets the eye.

Here is the King and Queen of England and the circle above them:

Circle & Triangle

incidentally this is a whole different subject of the British Royalty, the reason they call them the royal family comes from Egypt, Osiris, Isis and Horad were the original trinity of Egypt referred to as the Royal family, that where they get the royal, because of the triangle, pyramid of Egypt, when Gods son Horad rising, so there is nothing holy about these people at all. When the King of England becomes King the archbishop of Canterbury, listen to what the Archbishop has the King to say at the revelations ceremony, the Archbishop would say "you are now being crowned King of England for Jesus Christ, you are sitting on the throne of David for Jehovah, the god of the old testament you are in fact messiah waiting for Arsilo who is waiting for the messiah to come back, so you are going to rule Gods kingdom until Jesus comes back," that is what the King is told. The King of England sits on the throne of the God of the Old Testament for Jesus Christ, he represents God's Kingdom, and we understand that God's Kingdom is going to unite the world and a wonderful paradise, and therefore England is the United Kingdom. It is very interesting when you know where royalty comes from, and they believe that they are a holy family and God put them there, but the whole thing is based on Egypt, pyramids, triangles, and El Salvador has the triangle and they have the circle and triangle:

incidentally, there is a thing called a fridgeon capability, it is a crop that the old French illuminati freemasons wore when they overthrew the French monarchy and the French revolution, you probably read about it in school about the French revolution and the French government and they wore crops, they were like stocking caps, they were red stocking caps and it stood for fridgeon capability, and it goes back to the ancient Roman societies in ancient Rome. The triangle is within the circle even in Nicaragua and El Salvador; incidentally those are the 2 countries that we had a lot of trouble with war down in Central America, because of the symbol here:

This is what is causing the war, that symbol in the middle; it is called fridgeon capability. Here is another symbol of freemasonry on the Bible you will see the cross and the crown:

the cross and the crown of course is the cross is Jesus within the crown of salvation, if you go back to freemasonry you will see the cross and the crown. The cross and the crown is actually on a chart of freemasonry, the Scottish and York right, within 2 rights of freemasonry in America, the 2 most important are the Scottish and York right, the York right comes from England and it comes out of York, England and the Duke of York, Prince Andrew is the Duke of York, The York rite freemasons came to America, when America was founded the first thing they did when the Colombians came over, the York Right Freemasons came over and they set up what they call New York and New York is the empire state and that is why they have the Empire State Building. They are the empire state of the new world, it is the new world empire state and the empire strikes back, because it is symbolism. They have the 1st, 2nd and 3rd degree freemasons, that is why when the cops pick you up or if you are in court and the prosecutor gives you the 3rd degree, it is because the police is a Masonic order, and they wear the Masonic symbols of power on their arm; that is why they are called armed forces, because they use their arms. Here are the 3 layers of freemasonry:

it is 1st, 2nd and when you get to be a 3rd degree freemasonry, you either go to the Scottish Right or the York Right, the Scottish right is referred to as the Egyptian Right:

everything that teaches and believes is based on Egypt, or you can go into the York Right and they teach and believe is based on the old York order which is supposed to be called Christian.

British rite

So you have the Royal Arch Masons, it is really important and you have the cross and the crown again, the order of the red cross is one of them and here is the Order of Malta, when you give money to the red cross, remember where you are giving it to; it is going to the Masonic Order, and incidentally the red cross can go behind enemy lines, they are part of the war, so that is why they can go behind enemy lines and you can't, they operate on both sides, they are part of the establishment. So we have Royal Arch Masons with the triangle and the Red Cross and the Order of Malta. Bush went to Island of Malta to have a summit and it is on top of a mountain and the pyramid is the old mountain of God. Here is the cross and the crown and the Star of David with the Masonic handshake:

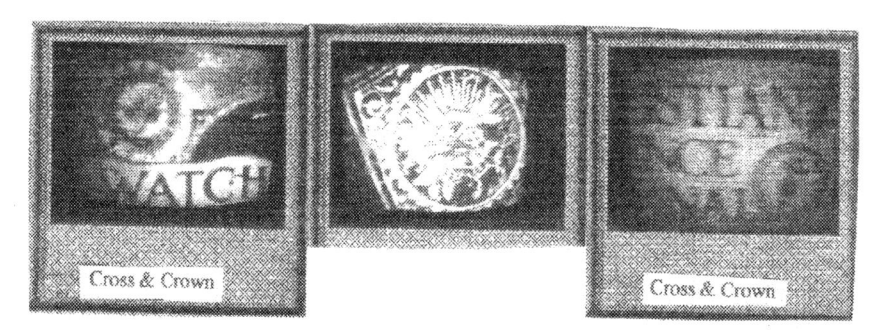

Cross & Crown   Cross & Crown

and here is the Masonic Order with the secret society of the Jehovah Witnesses:

the Jehovah Witness had no idea that the man that founded their order was a York Right freemason and he was financed out of England, his money came from England to start an order called British Israel freemasonry, he is nothing more than a Masonic conspirator to help the masters in England to take over our banking systems and our government, so that means for everybody to crawl on their knees and wait for God kingdom and think Jehovah is coming to save you, don't bet on it. Cross and the crown are found in many churches, they are like catalogs for different religious symbols.

Just remember when you go to different churches and you see the cross and the crown, just know they don't represent anything and there is nothing holy about it:

and remember they represent a very powerful secret society, the same people that are printing your money are directing the churches, freemason order, Christian Science, cross and the crown. Mary Becker Eddy's husband was a freemasonry in Germany, he was connected to the cross and the crown, the York Right he favored everywhere.

Some people think that these things in churches means holy and they have no idea where they came from and what they mean. And the church's ring is a commitment to Christ and whether they have a Masonic symbol on it.

They have night doctors that are freemasons that are referred to as night hospitalors, they are the ones that have control over the health in America, it is the American Medical Association and the American Health Association all hospitals come under the night hospitalors,

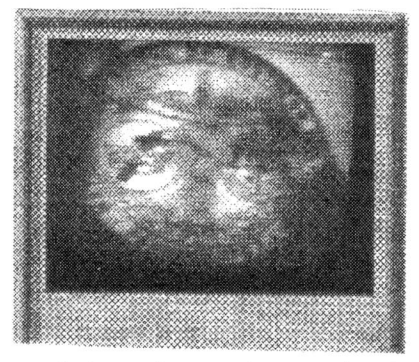

so when you hear all the crying on the news by the politicians talking about the cost of medical care, and what they are saying is that the hospitalors need some more money, so they are jacking up everything. We are being had by some very powerful secret societies that control our very life, everything we see everything we hear, our food is dominated by them, they are putting chemicals in our food and killing our people, they are beating people up, they don't care, these are fascist, they don't care a thing about you or nobody else. They have one thing in mind and that is to take control over the human rights, it is called the New World Order. Here is a community church on Van Vies Boulevard:

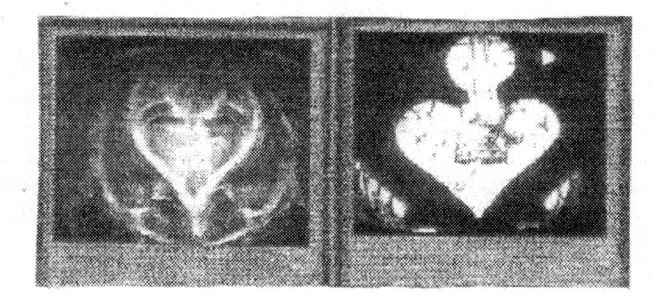

incidentally you will see pyramids all over it and triangles, and near the front and inside, you will see the cross and the crown, there is another one on Colorado Boulevard in Pasadena, it is a Presbyterian Church:

inside you see the same thing, a cross and a crown, and people think it is holy:

but what they don't understand it comes from the middle ages, these come from middle ages of secret societies of freemasons, this is a freemasonic emblem the colors, there is a reason for the blue, there are reasons for colors, there are reasons for the symbols, that have not got a thing to do with the lord and nothing to do with anything holy, the symbols come from the middle ages out of Germany and France and Spain and England and as they move into our country and try taking over our land and trying to convert us into slaves, they give us all of these emblems and symbols with their

Masonic order on them:

and they think they have pulled it off, but like Lincoln said, "you can fool some of the people some of the time and most of the people all the time, but you can't fool everybody all the time." Here is sovereign grand commander flag for world freemasonry:

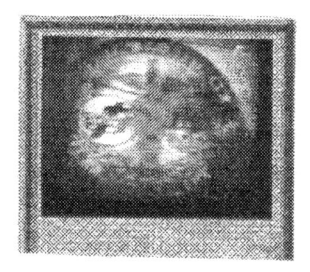

and on the supreme flag which is of course accepted all over the world, incidentally if you step into a court room today and if you see an American flag and if it has a gold trim around it according to International Marityn Emeralsy law, when a government is at war, it must fly its flag with a gold trim to show sovereignty in a point of war and a time of war, it is called Marshall Law in a time of war flags have gold trim which means before we were a country we were happy, we are at war, that gold means severity, we are at war, gold trim means Marshall Law, when you go into a courtroom and pay your fines or tickets or anything, you will see the American flag with the gold trim it means it is a military court, this is Marshall Law and they had the right to beat your brains out with a stick if they wanted to, this is not a civil court this is Marshall court under military control and the judges know that and most people don't understand that. On the world symbol for freemasonry flag you will see the snake biting its tail:

that has something to do with cult, but the word Ordo Ab Chao, you will see it in Masonic literature the double headed eagle:

incidentally the double headed eagle in freemasonry means the Masonic order is symbols by the eagle, incidentally we have an eagle as our symbol in America. The double headed eagle means: it is the Masonic order that has jurisdiction that has jurisdiction over us, the double headed eagle implies to according to Masonic literature and all their references that the Masonic order has jurisdiction over the western and the eastern world, so in Russia and China all the bad evil people over there as appose to western Europe and American England it is still the same game. Ordo Ab Chao; Ordo-out of kaos, so what we are talking about is people trying to organize, financing and directing chaos and for what purpose, to start a new order, to keep you frightened, scared and to keep you broke and on your toes, and while they keep you like this the chaos is still going on, they are instituting a new order and you did not even know it, in other words they are getting bad and they are going to get even badder. You will always see a double headed eagle in front of a Masonic lodging on a sword always on a sword, because they say real power comes from the sword and that is the way you create chaos with a sword, they are violent.

They used to have television shows on, one was called, "Get Smart," and if anyone tell you get smart, they are telling you that you are an idiot, get smart or wake up, get smart; what were the 2 signs of get smart; one was the chaos and the other was control, wake up get smart, this is what is going on here, it is a scam, so when you see all this laughing and the gangs killing, that is how its being planned, this government is planning gang warfare, they want the gangs to kill each other, that is part of sovereignty, it's incredible.

The California legislature in 1953 senate investigating committee and public by the state of California:

and this so called modern communism is apparently the same hypocritical and deadly way of conspiracy to destroy civilization is founded by the secret order of the illuminati in Bavaria 1776, May 1st. The world revolution conspiracy appears to be so well organized and ever continuing and ever on the alert to take advantage of every opportunity presenting itself so that the conspirators could create. The significant misconnection of early 1783 unsettled conditions and dissatisfaction some quarters of the American colonies, diverse of the matter were circulated amongst the colonial army to in spite the satisfaction of the rebellion, George Washington immediately called the army together and in addressing them he used this significant language, we are talking about 1783, George Washington said this, "my god, what can this writer have to do by recommending could he be a friend to the army, could he be a friend to this country, rather he not an insidious foe from emissary perhaps from New York." So George Washington already realized conspirators planning our demise operating out of New York, then the senate goes on to say, " it is plan that Washington believes the main center of this secret conspiracy, so far as this country was concerned to be located in New York and makes it his duty to make such a statement. So what they are talking about here is as far back as 1783, we have known what was going on." the next quote is," the recognition of May 1st 1776 is the founding date which is on the bottom of the pyramid on the dollar bill, 1776 it had nothing to do with founding this country in 1776, it has something to do with the founding of the illuminati in 1776, the recognition of May 1st is May Day that is military when the planes are going down or in trouble, they call it is a May Day call, may day means trouble, because these people are trouble, they cause chaos, violence, revolution throughout the world, blood shed in Afghanistan, Yugoslavia, anytime these people decide on want you that's trouble, may day, may 1st that is when the conspiracy was formed in 1776. Now the recognition of 1776 is the founding of this world revolution conspiracy and it is not difficult to understand when it is realized may day is frequently celebrated even in recent times by rioting and bloodshed in worldwide scales that is why the Soviet Union have their may day parade, because the Soviet Union was always going out killing people and murdering people and they would celebrate it on May 1st because what they are saying is that they are celebrating the world conspirators they are celebrating the world Masonic conspiracy that is financing the Soviet Union and as it says it is often celebrated even in times by rioting, that is why we had our last riot in Los Angeles and it was on May 1st, May Day. The thing is that it was set up in Los Angeles, the CIA and the Federal Government set up what we call the riot in Los Angeles, they set up these 4 guys, it was purposely set up because they knew these people were going to be mad and would riot, the whole thing was a set up that is why in wartime the Generals talk about the theater of war, specific theaters; the Atlantic Theater, the European Theater, theater implies as a act, it is a plan, it is just a theater, it's just entertainment, just like this, it is a theater of war in other words when you see all this violence, all the killing going on Czechoslovakia or in Yugoslavia, it has all been planned and what do you think the Pentagon is all about, they are planning how they are going to take over different countries, what they need from certain countries they are breaking the monetary Christians of the world and it is all been well planned and nothing like Roosevelt said, " there is nothing like this happening in politics." In issuing this manifesto the communist conspirator had believed that time had arrived in the aid of ignorant victims a worldwide takeover accomplished and there was not enough ignorant victims then and they expected to fail, the conspirators received the plan of the future of supplementing the longest fabric secret conspiracy every since May 1st 1776 with an incremented public campaign for victims among the ignorant of all nations and in an attempt to hide from view underlined hypocritical conspiracy existing since May 1st 1776 it was decided that public campaign the manifestations, the manifesto of 1848 writing the manifesto of 1848, the manifesto was wrote by Karl Marx, that is no such a thing, the communist manifesto was written in 1776 in Europe by a owner of the freemason called the illuminati and that wasn't until 1848 that they decided well we better tell everybody else that somebody else did it so they came up with Karl Marx doing it in 1848, no way. What we call communism is nothing more than a plan for the banking elements in England and America to divide the world between two divisions, to divide the world into the East and the West first you can have war, but you got to have war and chaos before you can bring control, that is why the United States financed Adolf Hitler, the United States financed the Soviet Union, it is called the Soviet Union not because it is a Union of State it is because it was a unionized and a labor international organization with the International Workers of the World, which because they wanted to unionize our labor, the company union the Soviet Union, they wanted to unionize labor with control over monetary and labor systems and now you can have war with each other and you got control over them, these people are very smart, they just stuck together. George Washington says, "I have heard much of the dangerous plan of the illuminati, it was not my intentions to doubt that the doctrines of the illuminati and the principles of the gothamanism had not spread in the United States and the masons and the illuminati and the United States, on the contrary no one is more truly satisfied than I am, so he is saying you don't have to tell me what is happening in New York because I already know. In the masons and the illuminati, George Washington's writing says, individual freemasons of them, I don't believe all freemasons in the whole world are evil, I don't believe all freemasons in the whole world are bad, but I know what they are talking about when you say there is a secret conspiracy operating out of New York and in America and in the world, nobody is more truly convinced of that than I am, of course there is a lot of ignorant people in freemasonry that don't know any of them, but that individual of them may have done it, Washington is saying the idea I meant to convey is that I did not believe that the lodges of freemasons in this country had all societies endeavored to propagate diabolical tenants of the first illuminati or the principles of balata if they are successful to separate them but that there are individuals in the freemasonic order who may have done that or that the founder or instrument of play found the democratic societies of the United States later to be known as the democratic party, the founder or the instruments employed that found the democratic party of the United States may have had the objects in mind and actually had the separation of the people from their government in view is to evident to be questioned, what he saying is that the democratic party was founded by a secret society of freemasons that had one thing that they wanted to do and that is to divide the people from their government because before on their republican form of government the people had total control because they were sovereign under a democratic system when you elect a democrat they were already had the idea of separating people from their government, you just elect some airhead here and send him to Washington and what you don't know is that this person is not even allowed to run for office unless he is one of them, so they have to be a part of the illuminati to run for senate or some other office, if you don't belong to the right freemason, you ain't going no where, period.

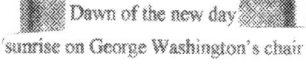

Here is a congressional report from the congressional hearings on steps to a British union against union, steps to a British union a world state an international strike. It is talking about a one world order, a world state an international war, this document is 28 pages long and page 13, it has the great seal of the U. S. you will find on the dollar bill you will find the exact same symbol for the British Israel world federation movement, the symbol is also carried in literature of organizations promoting a world government and world religion, at the bottom of circle surrounding the pyramid you will find the words Novus Ordo Seclorum this is the new order that was advocated by Clinton and Roosevelt several hundred years ago, so this is a symbol of a thing called the British Israel World Federation, it is a connection between England and America and the Masonic orders of both and they put them together, that is why they we say again that England is God's Kingdom, the United Kingdom, there is difference but a lot of people don't know this, there is a difference in being a British and English, Brit come from a Hebrew word meaning a covenant and is comes from Hebrew meaning man, British means a covenant man, man of the covenant what is covenant, new covenant God's covenant for a kingdom through Christianity through God's kingdom, the United Kingdom, the British and the British with America are involved in something called British Israel Freemasonry and all these dopes in Washington D.C. and these conspirators in Washington D.C. are nothing more than front men for a very powerful secret society preparing us to accept something that is called God's Kingdom, remember Armageddon, the end of the world, Jehovah Witnesses, the Mormons Church the end of the world, you better do your homework, there is something going on here. The state of is a legal term according to international Maritime Emeralty Law, that is why we have a state of Israel, it is not a country or a nation it is called a state of Israel, because it was set up as part of our federal system, it was set up in 1948 by the United States and England and it was referred to the International Maritime Emeralty Law, the state of Israel because it was a actual state of the federal system of America so you better figure out why too.

Here is a symbol taken from a freemasonic book:

Catholic church/knights of Malta Cross & Crown | cross & crown/knights of Malta | cross & crown/knights of Malta and here is the fires of revolution in trouble anarchy the causing of fire they call it in freemasonry, the revolutionary trouble and here is the with the Masonic and underneath it you have 3 contingences of fascist of freemasonry always at war with each other, you have the pope:

here is a Jewish freemasonic movement founded in the middle ages of 325 by constancy it is a freemasonic political movement.

The pope wears the little yamaka with the cardinals, they wear the telets and every symbol and emblem and the Catholic Church are nothing but Jewish freemasonry. The Roman freemasonry symbols you will see a lot of it in the movie Godfather 3, a lot of this stuff you will see in the movie are symbols of Roman freemasons operating the Vatican's and incidentally the guy that directed those films Francis Ford Coppa's father was a don of the mafia in the city of Corleon, Italy, his father was a don of the mafia, that is how he could make a movie and know so much about the mafia and how they work, and he is getting this money to make these movies from secret society and fraternal orders that are the powers behind our government. So we got the Vatican's, the Knights of Malta and the King of England:

they are all working up the fighters of trouble all over the world. Here is the Pope with the Yamaka:

all of these people are on their knees in front of the Pope, it is not because they are Catholic, it has to do with the fact that who he represents, he represents a very powerful secret society to as the Knights of Malta and the world freemasonry, there is something we call today, an unwritten code of ethics among the thieves, it may be the east coast family or the west coast family, but when you meet there is a certain respect for each other, the eastern nation, they respect that he represent a very powerful secret society of the west, and it doesn't mean can't go to war or we can't kill each other, but this is a state affair, so we are all on our knees and the symbols here:

Catholic church/knights of Malta

the stripes going over the shoulder are Masonic emblems, they always represent who you are in the Masonic spectra of things in world freemasonry, that is why they killed John Kennedy too, because the pope, the freemasonry in this country was afraid John Kennedy wasn't no joke and was going to start a catholic dynasty in America, and one thing they are not going to have is a catholic dynasty, and every time you told Kennedy he had more kids, he has sons all over, congress, senator and everywhere else, and there is a Kennedy doing something every time you turn around, so somebody decided to take Kennedy out. It is interesting that all the stuff around Kennedy's assassination is just filled with secret society and fraternal orders and all you have to do is see JFK and you know there is something going on here.

Here you got the knights of Malta and Nazi soldiers with Adolf Hitler:

knights of Malta   knights of Malta

Adolf Hitler was connected with the Vatican's, the Vatican's signed in ordinance with Adolf Hitler and that is why Mussolini, Hitler and the Pope were the enemies of Jewish freemasonry in America, that's why if they kill a few Jews in Europe, who the hell cares, that is why Hitler was killing Jews, because the Vatican's was an opposing branch of freemasonry which is a gentile Roman branch of freemasonry and which is why Rome, Mussolini of Italy joined together with Adolf Hitler because they were trying to reestablish what is called an Arian system of laws and science of the world as opposed to the new world order in America. So when you see all of these things happening on the world scale it is not just happening it is happening for a reason for all of this stuff.

Here are the Mounty officials:

knights of Malta

knights of Malta

they look like some of the people that run this country, and sometimes they look like governors and senators and whatever. Here is an emblem, this is the Knights of Malta, and they all wear the Knights of Malta symbol:

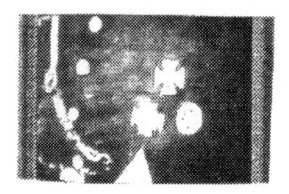

the Masonic order of Malta, Roman freemasonry, but then down here is the military order of Malta, incidentally when you see the round circle with the swatsicle, swatsicle was an old Arian Hindu symbol for the sun, like the Egyptians had Horad where the ancient Arians had the swatsicle for the sun, incidentally the swatsicle and the sun for the Arians and the Buddhist, the broken light was the opposite way, Hitler in voted them and went the opposite way, the Arians had it going clockwise, it meant something spiritually, Hitler broke the legs and made it go backwards, which meant it is going back to the east instead of going west, so he was reestablished in the old Arian empire on the ancient eastern occultism. Now all of this has to do with secret societies to inverts the movement.

This Knights of Malta religious emblem here is interesting because when you enlarge it you will see that it is the same one that was shown earlier. You will see 2 circles, there is an outside circle and an inside circle. It is in Pasadena, First Congregational Church in Pasadena, and the religious Knights of Malta emblem is on a church in Pasadena.

On all churches you will find a pointed arch on the doors and the windows:

the pointed arches represent the female, and that is why they don't allow women to be priest of a church because its philosophy is what we call Roman Catholic or Western Christian Civilization based on the female arch and the man wears the robe, which is a female dress, priest wear the dress because of spirituality in the ancient world, according to the ancient world spirituality was all in the hands of female not the males, men were never thought to be of a religion or spiritual teachers, they were the ones that went out and raped and killed and murdered and brought in the food and the women were the ones that brought civilizations to the males, you need the female to civilize society. The priest with the long dress is representing female wisdom, and with female wisdom beneath is the male.

We now get to York Right freemasonry and here is the Masonic square or the Knights of Malta crock.

Cross & crown/knights of Malta

Israel is making a wailing wall, it has to do with symbolism which goes back to Solomon's Temple, it was the symbol and the home of the Knights of the Templem, that is why Steven Spielberg has the Jedi Knight and the Empire Strikes Back, incidentally in the Masonic Folklore you will see the spiritual connection of the freemasons of the York rights and God was a little spiritual creature they call Yoda, it has to do with Knights of Malta, there is another thing from the Knights of Malta the 33rd degree freemason with the Malta. Here is the same one on Masters of the Universe:

Empire knights of Malta/religious | knights of Malta | knights of Malta

Now they want to go after the universe, Masters of the Universe, they had a blonde head and Arians, remember Hitler was a blonde head Arian, Knights of Malta, Catholic Church, they killed Jews, hey they are all connected. Here are the Knights of Malta again and I am talking about it because you will see it in fire departments, police departments, the Knights of Malta, because the Fire and Police departments and health departments, Military and everybody else's department because they are all Masonic the whole thing, we are in the hands of a very powerful secret society and we call it law and truly it is nothing more than secret societies who have totally taken us over and we just go along to get along with everything because we are too ignorant and too frightened. The Knights of Malta are freemasonic order coming out of the old Roman empire which has the collective power of the old world of Europe, Europe was dominated by Rome and so the Knights of Malta is the symbol for a Masonic Order coming out of the old world order of Europe and it was called "the Knights of Malta," and because it goes back to an old priesthood on the island of Malta, Malta was a symbol many, many, many years ago, over two thousand years ago in the Roman empire. There are certain places in our country that are called hot spots for occultism and the Roman Empire Malta, the island of Malta was a place where most people are really off the wall out there, they really got strange stuff going on out there, Malta was always a symbol for occultism, an innocent world and so the Romans had what they call the Knights of Malta.

The illuminati is a relatively new phenomenon in freemasonry, it came in 1776 with Adam Whitesok, but what the illuminati was, was nearly a correction in freemasonry, there was the Roman world and the Roman domination of Europe freemasonic order was the coming out of England, Spain, France coming of what is called the York Right or Scottish Right freemasonry. England, Spain, France coming into America from a new world order, but above them but of the 2 orders, the eagle with the double head implying that both sides, but the new world order and the old world order are being dominated by a 3rd one, and that is where James Bond novels come from, because there is the 3rd power over the 2, and the 3rd is controlling both of them, and that is the illuminati, and they don't mind using both because they remember that America is a York Scottish like country, and they have symbols of freemasonry. They will explain what the symbols stand for and what they mean and how they got here and why they allow them to be used, and they all are working together for the same goal, the same goal is to create chaos, to have Adolf Hitler fight the United States, to have Russia fight America, and to have China fight, and all of this stuff is coming from a higher Masonic order. They asked a man, "who is this spectra, there is a 3rd power group and they put the east and the west to war, and he said, "England and America and the western world and the eastern world are aware of a 3rd power in the world that put the 2 together and they are operating out of Switzerland," and that is where the big boys live and that is why people don't bother them. There is a big building in Switzerland and it is a perfectly round building and enormous in size and it is divided into an equal triangle and 1/3 of the building, you have to fly over it and see it and it is in a symbol of the peace symbol, the peace symbol was in the "y" symbol. The 1/3 of that building is the world headquarters for the United Nations and the other 1/3 is the world bank international monetary fund and the other 1/3 is the world headquarters of freemasonry of Masonic world Congress, so you got the Masonic world Congress, world government, United Nations and the world bank, so they put it all together so you don't have to go out for coffee and you can all work together and it is incredible.

Here again is the pope with the Jewish yamaka:

there is a reason the pope wears the yamaka, it is a Jewish head thing, it has nothing to do with God, it has to do with Jewish freemasonry, reason why he is called a cardinal is because cardinal means a hinge on the door, that is what the cardinal means in Latin, a hinge on the door, pope comes from papa which is Latin which means the door to the mystery, he is the one you must go through to open up the mystery of God, for he is the door he is the hinge, the cardinal is the hinge for the door and that goes all the way back to Babylon, the old ancient Babylonian mystical religion.

Here is a freemasonic document that shows some of the different visions of freemasonry throughout Europe and what they mean and how all these guys are all connected from England to France and Italy and Spain, and how it is all being orchestrated. It shows some of the different concurrent orders of freemasonry and some of the different symbols they use throughout Europe, and it looks like the pope's headdress. These are all accouchements for Juddism, it is the Ark of the Covenant and the mercy sea and here is the

Jewish high priest wearing the headdress the same wore by the pope, so we are talking Jewish and not talking about Roman Catholic.

Different masons throughout Europe

Here are some symbols of the different departments of freemasonry:

and the screen of the high priest and king, and for the high priest you have the pope's headdress and the pope is the high priest of freemasonry and the king of England is too, but there is a wall between the king of England; Henry the 8th had a falling out with the pope, and King Henry said to the pope, "I don't like the way you are doing things here, you are hanging out too much with the wrong kind of people and so we all Knights of the order of York are not happy with you and so we are going to break it off, we don't want you ruling England anymore and so from here on out we are going to King of the Kingdom." On the pope's symbol there are always 2 keys on the bottom of it and that is where they get the Florida Keys from, because if you think about it the Florida Keys is home for the most powerful people the world has ever known, and they got a whole thing down there and if you understood how many millions of dollars were spent just building that highway, that is an astronomical for the military and the military just laid it all out and the military and if you go down that highway, it has the most beautiful highway going way out as far as the eye could see and how much does that cost? And how come you put it out there, for who, it is out in the middle of nowhere and it is not little, it is a big beautiful highway, because there are families that live out there and you always see the presidents going out there, that is because these guys have power and that is all that is out there is people with power by themselves, these guys are absolutely horrendous, they got a thing going that will not stop and we have no idea in the world what is going on, that is why they call it the Florida Keys. And again within the triangle of freemasonry, you have the pope's hat, here is the breastplate of righteousness, for the Jewish high priest of Juddism, the freemasonic apron, the fluid ali which is the symbol of France, the symbol of sex, the male and the female and the pope's headdress.

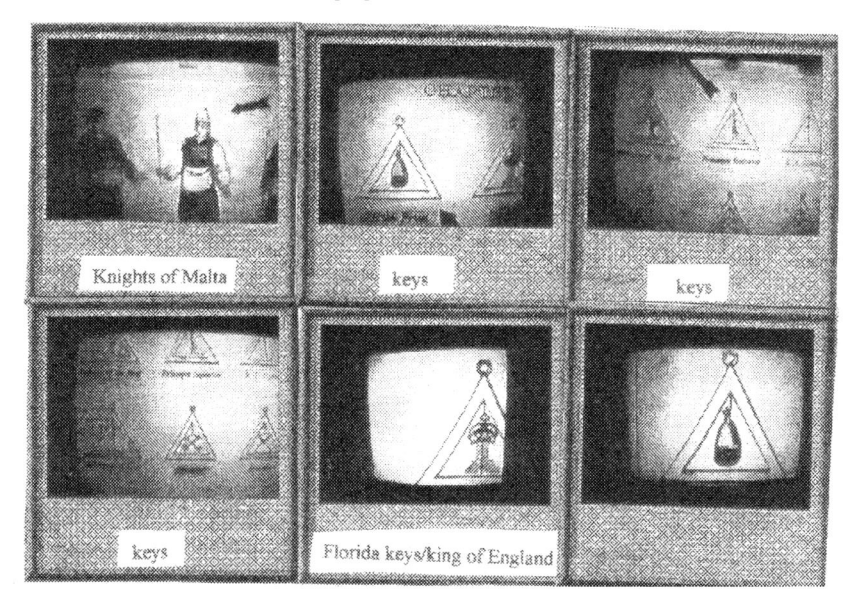

Knights of Malta	keys	keys
keys	Florida keys/king of England	

Here is another Masonic apron and on the apron you will see the King of England, the Pope:

Black robe/Masonic square	Dawning of a new day/the sun rising over the east

incidentally that is why when you go to college, you get out of high school you wear a black robe the same thing the priest wear, the same black robe that the judge wear and the square you wear on your head, is called a marker board, it is the square of freemasonry, so if you go to church and you do things right and stay in line you are a square.

Here is what we call the royal arch freemasonry:

Keystone royal ark

and the stone that holds the 2 together are called a key stone, that is why Pennsylvania is called the keystone state, because Pennsylvania is where the Constitution was signed and these guys put this whole thing together, the keystone state where the keystone was started between the 6 and 6 and 1 found in the middle which makes 13, the 13 colonies, the keystone state, again it says for the royal arch chapters, note the headdress of the principles, and again you have the King of England and the Pope.

Knights of Malta | keys

This is called the 60 degree of freemasonry and there is a "G" in the middle for geometry:

Dawning of a new day/the sun rising over the east

and the reason it is like that is because the triangle is pointed down and the triangle pointing up and if you cross through there and then it is called the star of David, that is why it is that way and that is according to the Masonic books, it is actually a take off on the star of David, triangle up and triangle down, it is a 60 degree square, and on them they always have the ribbon, that is called a 90 degree square and you have to keep that in mind because that is a Masonic square, and here it is:

Masonic Square | *Masonic Square*

So when you see these certain kind of people they are wearing the square of freemasonry, and it is inappropriate because they are worshipping a Masonic God.

Black robe/Masonic square | *Black robe/Masonic square*

Here is St. Louis at Jerusalem, according to Masonic history;

Saint Louis of Jerusalem captured Jerusalem for Knights of Templar

the man who first casted Jerusalem for the Knights Templar was St. Louis, for they honor in St. Louis with the Royal Arts, the Royal Arts Degree of Freemasonry.

Royal ark

And there is nothing happening by chance because the economics in this country have no problems, so there are no problems with anything in this country. Here is something called the Summit of the Arts:

Royal ark

and it comes from the state department bulletin and here is a meeting:

Paris, France the summit of the arch

showing all the top criminal families; the Germans, Americans, and Margaret Thatcher, and these are all the heads of state in the western world, and they would take a picture in front of the pyramid in France:

Paris, France the summit of the arch

and anytime you have a great war or anything, they would have a past peace conference, Vietnam and Korea always go to Paris, because Paris is the home of the French Grand Opening Freemason. Why do they call it the Summit of the Arts? There is a freemasonic library that will show you how it is connected with religion; and they got Masonry, Mormonism and Freemasonry.

Mormons are founded by, financed by, directed by and organized by the freemasons; Joseph Smith and Brigham Young; the leaders of the Mormon Church, are both 32nd degree freemasons of the Scottish Rights. Here is another book; The Relationship of Mormonism and Freemasonry, Mormonism of the Freemasons, Freemasons and the book of Mormons, that is why in Utah we have Zion's, Zion National Park.

Zion National Park was a great white zone, incidentally it is not a black zone, its a white zone, and that is why America is ruled by the White House, not the Brown House or the Blue House but the White House and that is because England is ruled from what is called the white hall, White Hall is a symbol for power. And the people that are running this country are the most powerful criminals there are.

The Masonic Orders of Fraternity, the direct decent of the essential program of the etecleric schools was entrusted to groups already well condition of the work, the Gerald Trade Union protective of societies have been internally strengthened by the introduction of a new learning, the advancement of the plan required an enlargement of the boundaries of the philosophical overstate, a world prepantity was needed sustained by a deep and broad program of education, according to the method, there is a method to this education that we are getting. Friendship Fraternity could not immediately include men, but could unite the activities of certain kinds of men no matter of racial background or religious beliefs or the nations they dwell; here is the point, these were the men of coordination, though suns of tomorrow whose symbol was the blazing sun rising over the mountains of the east. What it is talking about is that the conspiracy already had knowledge that the Gild Trade Union similar to but never in societies were perfect ground for control, so you set up the red cross, you set up the painters union, you set up these unions but never in societies; this man set them all up to sensibly protect the people, when in fact they are being organized and directed to control the people, and we can't explain this conspiracy to everybody, and we can't count in everybody in on this, but we could unite certain kinds of men as long as we understand what is going on here, we can unite these different organizations together and the symbol for these men; the suns of tomorrow was; a blazing sun rising over the mountains of east, while it is difficult to trace the elements of a pattern, never intended to be obvious, the broad shape of a design is dimly apparent, the invisible impact, it has always been intended to be difficult anyway, because on the inside you know there is a design but on the outside you cannot tell that there is an design, here is where they are getting this from, this is from the old Babylonian Mythology, the sun rise the Gods appear from the mountains of the east, here is God's son rising over the mountains of the east;

dawn of the new day

Dawning of a new day/sunrise

and that goes all the way back to Babylon; in Hebrew Theology the sun rising is the light of Mt. Sinai, the sun rising over the east. The sun rising on Hebrew Jewish Freemasonry, here it is in Kabala and here on the back on chapter 9 is called the way of one who is caught between the suns of a dime and a dawning day, the way of the one who is caught between the suns means, there are 2 suns, one is going down and a new sun coming up, the old sun of the old world order, Rome is going down, Vatican's, Europe is the old sun and it is going down and there is a new sun coming up on America, the dawn of a new day for America and it is going to be the King of the World now. A dime and a dawning day; George Washington said here is his chair:

Fugian cap of liberty

sunrise on George Washington's chair

where he signed all of his documents, and in that chair he said, "But now at length I have the happiness to know it is a rising and not a setting sun." Here is a book by James Billington;

it is about from its earliest origins in a cult freemasonry to the allegedly scientific marchism. In the encyclopedia on Russia and other side is the flag and the coat of arms, the National Coat of Arms talks about the rising of the sun is a symbol of the dawning of the new day of communism:

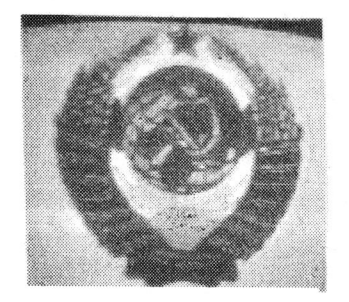

this symbol came out for the Soviet Union in 1930 late 30's mid to late 30's, it originally came out that time, in New York we have the dawning of a new day of communism, it is connected with the New York world fair and the coming of the Soviet Union, and the half dollar:

dawning of a new day for communism

and here it says, "here is moving toward the dawn of a new day," the sun rising for us to put communism over there it is rising through us now," now we are coming towards communism, we call it democratic, the people's democratic republic of Cuba, the people's democratic republic of Romania and now we have the people's democratic republic of America and all marchist communism is the same as old Roman fascism, it is all sasolatarian dictatorship, period.

dawn of the new day

Here is the founder of Jehovah Witnesses, and he is telling everybody the new day is dawning and preparing all the Jehovah Witnesses for the dawn of the new day.

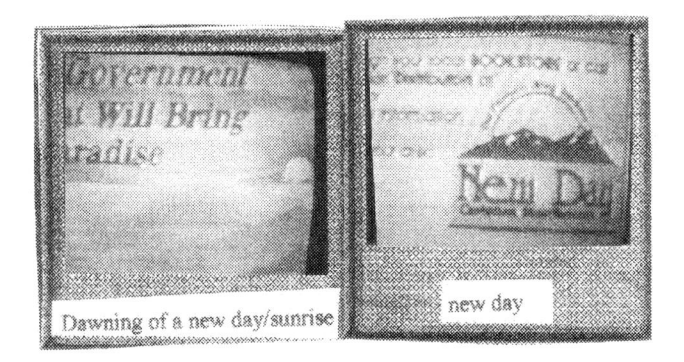

Dawning of a new day/sunrise *new day*

Here is the watchtower in the society of Pennsylvania Jehovah Witness with the sun rising over the mountains in the east:

Dawning of a new day/sunrise

the Christian materials called the new day with sun rising over the mountains of the east, and people have no idea that this stuff is being manipulated and presented to them and they have no idea in the world, and they are out there preparing the world to accept God's kingdom and they never realize that the symbols of channel 40 are Masonic and all their leaders are all freemasons.

Richard Nixon set the coin for himself:

Dawn of the new day/republic

and called it the new day for America, the new dawn of peace and that is what he did. Here is Liberia, the flag:

is a symbol for the rising sun, the sun withholds a new day, Romania, there symbol is the sun like the shell gas station, the sun rising over the mountains of the east, the rising sun expresses the promise of a new day, here is Mongolia, the horsemen on horses:

the sun rising over the mountain stands for the nations advance towards communism, Malaui, is the red sun,

Malawi added the sun symbolizing dawning of a new day for Africa and it was, there were a lot of killing over there, and Afghanistan,

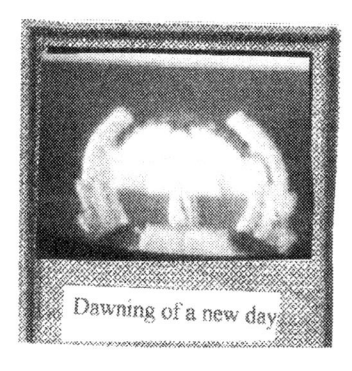

PROBLEMS OF THE WORLD

the dawning of a new day for them and they killed a lot people over there too, and on school rings, college rings: a new dawning the sun coming up is on rings in high school and the sun rising coming up on the mountains of the east, they control education, religion, part of the fire department, police departments, they all are in control of the world we live in, it is the only game in town. Behold a new dawn, the people that wear these rings have no idea what that means.

A recurrent model for revolutionaries, an early romantic young Karl Marx, the Russians of Lenis time was Prometheus, who stole fire from the Gods for the use of mankind. Here in New York at Rockefeller center we have the Prometheus fountain, the Masonic square of freemasonry, that is why when they have the Olympics they run around with the torch; it is the torch of Prometheus, the statue of Liberty holds the torch of Prometheus, it is a symbol for the age of enlightment or the illuminati; the illuminated ones.

The United Nations Postal Office used to have the red, white, and blue and now they just have the simple blue because it is a symbol for Israel:

this particular blue has since become known as U.N. blue, it comes from the old Grand Lodge of freemasonry. That is why the United Nations is blue, and when you are in college you get a degree, because these people teach you what they want you to know, they teach you how to earn a living and not a living to earn and they teach you how to think, and that is why when you get out of college they call you an alumni, they illuminate you, you are illuminated by the powers that be as long as you stay square, you will do alright.

So read your history and find out what is really going on in the world today, and wake up America, life isn't never just about you, life is about what you see in your eyes and if you can see then you have the will and the money, I think that is what God is going to judge you by, what you could've stopped or avoided and if you can stop one death, then you are automatically going to heaven and it says if you risk your life for another then you are in, so however life turns out, wake up America, this is your world, there is only one and after this, there would be no more.

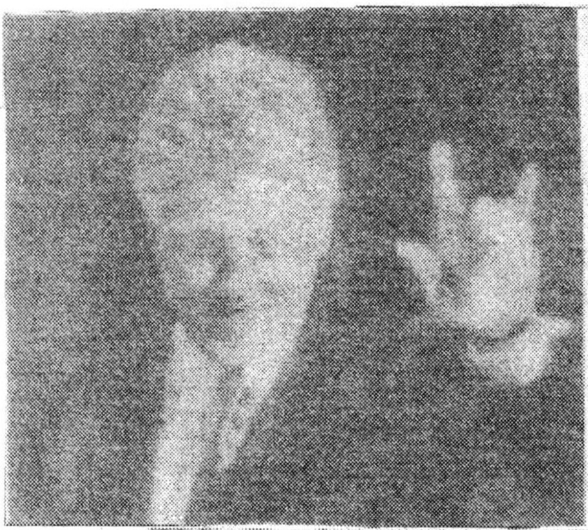
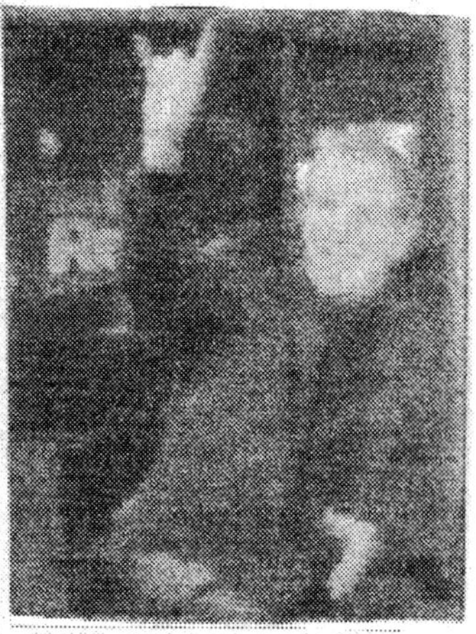
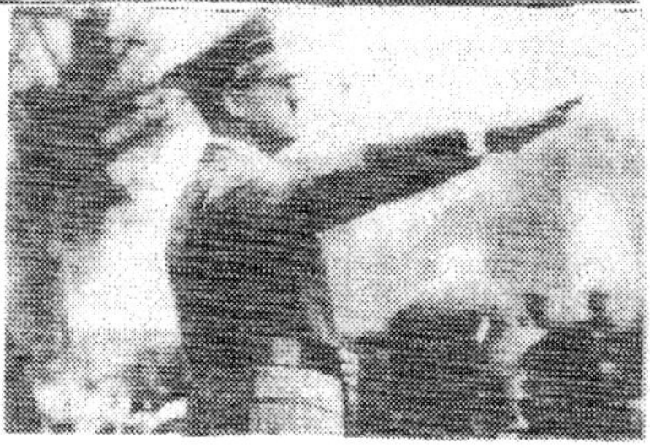
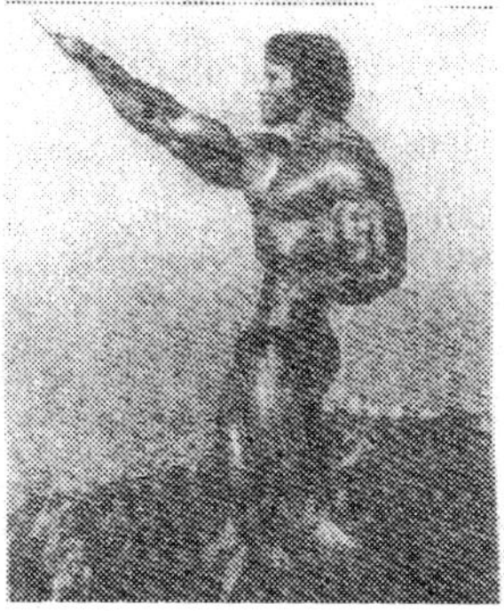

A newspaper article I was really concerned about.

U.S. military seeking answers to suicide rate of troops in Iraq

WASHINGTON - U.S. soldiers in Iraq are killing themselves at a high rate despite the work of special teams sent to help troops deal with combat stress, the Pentagon's top doctor said Wednesday.

Meanwhile, about 2,500 soldiers who have returned from the war on terrorism are having to wait for medical care at bases in the United States, said Dr. William Winkenwerder, assistant secretary defense for health affairs. The problem of troops on "medical extension" is likely to get worse as the Pentagon rotates hundreds of thousands of troops into and out of Iraq this spring, he said.

Both situations illustrate the stresses placed on the troops and the military's health system by the war in Iraq.

Suicide has become such a pressing issue that the Army sent an assessment team to

Iraq late last year to see if anything more could be done to prevent troops from killing themselves. The Army also began offering more counseling to returning troops after several soldiers at Fort Bragg, N.C., killed their wives and themselves after returning from the war.

Winkenwerder said the military has documented 21 suicides during 2003 among troops involved in the Iraq war. Eighteen of those were Army soldiers, he said.

That's a suicide rate for soldiers in Iraq of about 13.5 per 100,000, Winkenwerder said. In 2002, the Army reported an overall suicide rate of 10.9 per 100,000.

The overall suicide rate nationwide during 2001 was 10.7 per 100,000, according to the federal Centers for Disease Control and Prevention.

By contrast, two U.S. military personnel killed themselves during the 1991 Persian Gulf War, although that conflict only lasted about a month. The Army's recorded 102 suicides during 1991 for a rate of 14.4 per 100,000. The Army's highest suicide rate in recent years came in 1993, when the rate was

15.7 per 100,000.

The Marine Corps has the military's highest suicide rate. Last year the Marines' rate was 12.6 per 100,000. During 1993, the Marines' rate was 20.9 per 100,000.

In 1993, there was U.S. military action in Somalia and Haiti.

The military has nine combat stress teams in Iraq to help treat troops' mental health problems, and each division has a psychiatrist, psychology and social worker, Winkenwerder said. Of more than 10,000 troops medically evacuated from Iraq, between 300 and 400 were sent outside the country for treatment of mental health problems, he said.

The military prefers to treat mental health problems such as depression by keeping troops in their regular duties while they get counseling and possibly medication, Winkenwerder said. Less than one percent of the troops in Iraq treated for mental issues during an average week, he said.

The military also is working to solve the issue of soldiers awaiting non-emergency medical care. Since November, about 1,900 of 4,400 waiting for medical care have been treated, Winkenwerder said.

But the military expects more problems when tens of thousnds of troops are rotated in and out of Iraq this spring, Winkerwerder said. Many of those troops leaving Iraq may have to wait at various bases in the United States for medical treatment such as physical therapy for injuries, he said.

The Army is working to sign contracts with civilian medical providers and is bringing in more staff from the Navy, Air Force and the Department of Veterans Affairs to help, Winkenwerder said.

I wrote this 2 days after the war started in Iraq, and never mailed it.

To whom it may concern:

As it states in the Bible, the third war is the last war that will end the world. I feel that if you love your people the way you say you do, instead of dropping bombs overnight, do what you did in Afghanistan when you dropped food first and then dropped the bombs. And instead of dropping pamphlets telling the soldiers to surrender, drop pamphlets letting them know when food in coming. I found out on The History Channel that the U.S. sold Saddam Hussein and other countries the technology to make chemical warfare. So why not just offer to buy it back from him and give him and his sons exile to leave the country and let the U.N. come in and patrol the Iraqi soldiers that patrol the country and let the U.S. deliver food to them. And this time don't kill the devil, let the devil live so that we all could live.

The harder you work, the more they take.

Don't it feel like when you are broke, you have no friends or you have a debt that you can't get out of and people look at you differently. The trick is not to care, but you get so used to not caring, you forget what to care about. What if it is not your fault that you don't have any money? It is your governments fault who is controlled by the politicians who control your money and your life with your money by putting obstacles in your way so you cannot know that your life is controlled and your history is not being made but controlled. The trap of life states; that by not knowing who's controlling everything that take place in your life. Because of all the obstacles such as: child support, taking your kids to school, going to the doctor 4 or 5 times every other month, paying insurance for your car, watching your back wherever you go, worrying about your family getting out of jail so he or she can see their families and kids again.

They also control what you can afford to buy with your own money. While they get rich, your children see what's going on in front of them everyday while you are working hard trying not to loose your job.

Your children learn at an early age, that all it takes to survive is to eat and watch your watch your back. They learn at an early age because they think that's all it takes to survive in this world. You don't see it because you are working to pay your bills and keep food on the table. Why did they decide to throw people off of welfare, why not just the married couples and not the single parents? Why can't it be like I was raised, when someone was home with us and other working parent's children? Why do you think they don't give you the power to control what your kids do? That is the hardest obstacle they put in front of you, but they make you not care so much that you don't know where all the money went.

People are killing each other over change because they don't know where all the money is going. The politicians are playing war games with your life, and they are using your money to do it while the rich are getting richer and the poor are getting poorer. Nobody or nobody's child's life means anything to them. I've been in debt a lot of times, but it seems like the harder I work they just keep coming up with more debts you constantly hear about. Someone or someone's child dying, and they think more about watching your back, because your politicians are gambling with your life and your money. I seen Bush cry once and that was at the Twin Towers site. There are soldiers dying everyday and I don't see anybody crying about that.

110

Bush doesn't hide his abiding faith.

Just because innocent Iraqis are getting killed, our children are dying for them and the politicians are not crying over that.

What if everyone took the time to find out the things your child sees and feels everyday you would notice how smart they really are. Find out who has the most problems and you will find out the hard way what your child seen or heard was just by paying attention to adults. But you want your child to be smart so they could go to college or even be a hard worker. But they keep you so occupied and worried that you don't even know that you can change your future by just VOTING! You should be smart and VOTE for the person who cares about your children just as well as their own children. You have people out here that you have to watch and cannot trust so you push them away because you never know when they are going to feel life is just not worth living anymore. The rich that do love their kids and worry because they might go to school with the starving and bad community.

So they make the rich pay for their good lives, but they need more money so the rich can donate more money to the political campaigns and more money to play war games with your children's lives. They have your child dodging bullets all day everyday for the rest of their lives, and all it takes to change it is for the world to agree on what's more important, our children's future and living now or living like it is so easy for everyone and not care about anyone but yourself. They make you so worried about other stuff, that they make you not even care about how long the war will last so you can see your kids grow up. While you worry your kids cannot see a future or a life; the law and the politicians will not allow you to. And they don't want to tell you what they do when they see starving people in your hometown while they are campaigning.

They need to go to homeless shelters and see that their people and starving too. There is a lot of food for everyone, so why is there people starving in America? They want people to be scared of each other so they will not standup to know each other. The heartache and pain is put in your way so you cannot concentrate on making it, and there are people playing war games with the world's children.

They don't give the soldiers a way to protect themselves or even get seen by a doctor for weeks, and while all of this is going on, rich and poor kids are dying everyday for money. If everyone would VOTE for someone who cares and make sure that they stay in office, he could put our lives back together again. But you have to be the one to put him in office by VOTING, and not the one who got the biggest contributions or VOTED in by dead people. We have to pick the right person, someone who is satisfied with their lives and love everyone and not just certain people. The world is so separated, poor hate rich and the rich hate the poor. If you love the people, then you should help the people. Why do it seem like everywhere you go is being controlled? It is by your politicians and your own money.

You think you can't live without money, when all it takes to live is to eat. So America, let's get together and stop the end of the world by agreeing from the hearts and not the pockets, before it is too late. ONE VOICE, ONE MIND, and HEART: that is to live. You can do it because it won't cost you anything to VOTE. All these years with no war and the Americans were not even prepared, and I wonder where all the money over the years. I bet the politicians know because they play with it everyday and they don't shed a tear about that.

BRING HIM D

On a fund-raising trip for his 2004 re-election bid, B draws protesters outside a Riversi

To America, ONE HEART, ONE SOUL

Heaven is waiting for us all, and we can stop from all of us going at the same time.

TIME   *(Replace all Politicians)*

   IS

      LIFE

So wake up America, money only has the power you give it.

The poor people are not the only people who suffer, the rich suffer too because of the Political Decisions. The famous people have problems just as much or even worser than the poor people. They have problems such as where they can go is limited because of the Political Decisions that keep the poor and less fortunate unable to control their kids, because the law will not allow you to punish them in the way you think is necessary. They make it look like the rich hate the poor by making their neighborhoods look so run down and poor that only drug dealers and drug addicts live in the ghetto, but in reality they live everywhere. So they should not judge the rich over the poor, because GOD created us all.

The rich are paying all of this money for security and protection from what they call the POOR PEOPLE when there is rich people doing crimes just as well as the poor people, such as: murder, kidnapping, and robbing. And why they are paying all of this money for security and protection, they are laying of 200 police officers, so how are we going to protect ourselves or our children from those murderers, robbers, and pedophiles? They are keeping the ghetto poor and they rich afraid to go into the ghetto. So everyone needs to wake up and not just the poor people, because the politicians are controlling you and your money as well. The world would be a better place if everyone would see the light and unite as one. ONE HEART, ONE MIND, ONE SOUL and most of all ONE WORLD!!!

Why we are thinking about it, whatever happened to the money Bush had for Homeland Security?

There are 2 ways they control the rich and the poor with the laws they make. For example: if you get caught with 5 kilos of powdered cocaine, you would get 3 or 5 years in jail, but if you get caught with 1 kilo of rock cocaine, you could get 30 years in jail. But they say rock cocaine is more addictive than powdered cocaine. But I thought when you investigate drug dealers, you try to catch the Kingpin, so why does the supplier of the Kingpin get less time if you are trying to keep drugs off the street. Another is theft. The rich get more time than the poor people do. But the whole agenda is to keep the streets safe.

One of the world's biggest problems is that Bush promised us that he was going to make this world safer for Americans. He got a check signed just for that cause; to keep us safe. When Jane Campbell was elected mayor of Cleveland, she promised the same thing. There is money that is supposed to be for protecting us, but our Homeland Security is getting laid off. We will have to suffer because of that, and the families of the police force, firefighters, and the paramedics will have to suffer also. There is a threat of America being hit by terrorists again. We already have police on the force that are too old and cannot retire because they cannot afford to. And now they are laying off 200 police officers. But guess what, they are laying off first the ones that were hired last, so that means the police that need to retire will still be on the force.

At the beginning of the year of 2004, they are releasing over 2000 inmates out of jail that does not have anywhere to go and they will not have any medical insurance. These inmates that they are releasing, are the ones that been in jail for a very long time and when they are free, they probably will commit another crime so they can go right back to jail because that is what they are used to, and that will put our children's lives in danger everyday on their way to and from school. And since they are laying off firefighters and paramedics, what if someone's house catches on fire, who will put out the fire? And what if someone gets hurt, who will take him or her to the doctor if they cannot drive or have no one to take them to the hospital? Why are these people getting laid off when Bush got a check for Homeland Security?

When they do that, our world would not be safe anymore. How can the world survive without protection? When did the money start being more important than the lives of our children? It is hard to raise a child who sees no future because of what is going on around them, but you can show them one. And remember you only have one chance to raise a child, one chance only. ONE LIFE, ONE SOUL, and ONE HEART. The blood that keeps the world together is one color, so why is there so much hate because of the color of your skin or your religion? I don't care how you think you are different, we are all the same on the inside and we all need to see that we are all the same in GOD'S eyes. How much money you have should not mean anything, but they say, "money is the rule of all evil", but on your money is says, "IN GOD WE TRUST".

How is the state trying to protect us through the police force, when there are officers that are too old to be on the force? They can't afford to retire because their insurance is increasing and they can't afford to stay on the force because of their health. Now you tell me who is controlling the violence and the killings.

A man in Arizona worked for 20 years had to stop working because of his health; he has hepatitis C and Sclerosis of the liver. He went and applied for disability but he was denied because he hadn't worked in the last 5 years. They told him that if he divorced his wife he could be eligible for the benefits and medical coverage for his liver transplant. Now tell me is that fair. So now the government doesn't care about married working families.

The city donations come from the Political Campaigns, so the city that donated the most money was Manhattan, NY. They go by the zip code to know which cities donated the most money. Those cities get all of the donations and loans. Manhattan, NY already donated over 3.5 million dollars, over the yearly amount they have already been donating over the years. Bush already got over $712,000 already. So the rich that donate to the campaigns are buying their good living through the politicians and not the people or the cities that need it. So the politicians are controlling the poverty in every city with America's tax dollars. The problems of the world also control the stock market.

Tens of thousands of police are now wearing bullet proof vest made of zilon, that will deteriorate after 1 year and they are suppose to last for 5 years.

An elderly Olympic woman was fined 7 thousand something dollars for riding her bike through Cuba. The office that gave her the letter and the fine are suppose to be tracking down terrorists.

The LAPD signaled for a driver to stop because they though he was driving a stolen vehicle. They cuffed him very tightly and damaged his left hand and arm. Now he cannot perform his duties as a surgeon. They say it was racial profiling, because he was black and the officers were white.

The check that Bush has for Homeland Security was not used for it, a 21 year old college student proved that the money for Homeland Security was needed but was not used for it, because he put box cutters in a Southwest Airline bathroom.

One of Bush's highest campaign donators was Halliburton, with 1.6 billion dollars for the rebuilding of Iraq.

It is a law now that if you live in Public Housing, you have to do 8 hours of community service a month, even if you are disabled or elderly. If you don't do the 8 hours a month, you will get evicted. So they are saying volunteer or else. If you are paying rent or working less than 30 hours a week, you still have to do the community service. If you don't have a babysitter or any reason and you can't make it, you still will have to get evicted. Now you don't have to go to jail to do community service, you can be free and in no trouble and still have to do community service. This went into effect Oct. 1st.

There is only 1000 Cleveland Police in the city and the other 800 and Downtown in City Hall and the County is doing nothing, so Bob Beck wants all of them off their butts and back on the streets. When the reason for that is that downtown could not handle the streets. And he knows if they are on the streets they will quit.

The city council gets a 6% pay raise every year, while the Cleveland Police gets a 4% raise. They are taking the whole Cleveland Police raise away and the Cleveland Police asked why, and the city council told them that their raise is protected under a different law. And once the Police Dept. gets laid off, there will be no more follow up investigations; such as: Domestic Violence, Assault, Felonious Assault, No more Gang Units, No More Drug Units, Rape Investigations, No More Detectives to investigate anything under Felony 1's.

Jane Campbell's husband Hunter Morrison is the city planner for Youngstown. He used to be city planner for Cleveland. His brother own the construction company that is rebuilding I-90 all the way down to the turnpike. Campbell gave all the city council including herself, a pay cut, now that is what I call keeping the money in the family. She's giving the city council pay cuts, but yet and still she hired back the 2 police officers with a pay raise of 300 something thousand dollars a piece, that beat up the black guy and got fired. But there are mothers out there that cannot pay for daycare and they have to pay even if their children do not attend daycare for about a week or so. For example: I read in the paper that a young mother had to pay for her son not being in daycare for 1 week because he had to have a surgery. The money that Campbell gave to the 2 police could have went to daycares since they want people off of welfare so they can find a job.

I feel like this is a control trial to get a guilty plea from the jury.

To whom it may concern:

I am presenting this statement because I feel the defendant was not represented to the best of the law.

We pleaded for 3 days for the Defense Lawyer to use the tape recorder for evidence that states why the Defendant left his residence. There is also evidence that states these allegations were planned. The Defense Lawyer was not allowed to present all of his evidence that would have proved his innocence, but the prosecutor was allowed to present all of his evidence to prove the Defendants guilt, and I did not feel that was right. The Defense Lawyer did not cross examine the conspirator or the plantiff on the lies they were caught in. They both were caught in a lie stating that the ambulance did not show up, when the officer said that it did within 3-4 minutes. The officers that came to the conspirators residence did not do a thorough investigation as they were supposed to in a rape case. They subpoened the Plantiff's Social Worker to come to court, but they cancelled her to come after the allegations were made on how troubled a child the Plantiff really was. They should have subpoened the person she was on the phone with, because they could have heard something or the Plantiff saying no, like she stated she did. The officer told the conspirator to take the Plantiff to the hospital to get a rape kit, but she refused. The conspirator stated under oath that she was going to call the police when the Defendant got to her residence, after a disagreement about a cell phone and not the rape, but the Defense Lawyer did not cross examine her on that statement. There were different lies and statements that I wanted the Defense Lawyer to cross examine the conspirator on, such as: her stating that she had no contact with the Defendant after the allegations were made and there were witnesses that could prove otherwise. The Defense Lawyer could not cross examine her on that statement because they never came back. I asked the Defense

Lawyer the following day where they were, and he told me that they did not have to come back anymore. I also asked him if the evidence in the trial was not used, could it be used in the appeal? He told me no, and never related the message to his client. On other terms, I myself had to call the police on the conspirator several times because she would not leave our residence. The Prosecutor and the Defense Lawyer used my name several times, but did not use me as a witness, and I was there to be a witness. The Defendant and myself went down to the police stations several times to sign a statement right after the allegations were made. After the allegations were supposed to have been made, the conspirator came to our residence with 3 guys to jump the Defendant, not knowing that I was going to be there. A few days later they caught up with him and they jumped him. The Plantiff lied at the preliminary hearing about her age and she told 2 or 3 different stories. The prosecutor would not have had an closing arguement if the Defense Lawyer would've gotten the documents from the police officer who took down our statements, when we went to file a complaint on the conspirator. So if the Defendant was running, why would he go to 2 or 3 different police stations several times to do what he thought was right, and they never arrested him? Also, the Defense Witness and the conspirator both stated under oath that the Defendant went to the bathroom 4 different times, they also stated that he started going to the bathroom as soon as the lights went out,(they went out as soon as they arrived). Also they both stated that the Plantiff's father and brother were there for a while, but the Plantiff and the conspirator both stated that the Defendant started doing these things as soon as the father and the brother left. So how did this allegation take place 3 times after the father left is what I want to know?

But guess what, the Plantiff got sent back to the group home the following day. So if the Plantiff just got raped, why would the conspirator(her aunt) send her back the very next day? The conspirator neither the Plantiff told the Social Worker she was raped.

If she was scared as she stated she was, why would she ask her aunt after she came downstairs to tell her father goodbye, yet and still not tell anybody what supposed to had happened to her, to go back upstairs to use the phone in the same room where the alleged rape took place.

On the tape, the conspirator says on the 21st of August 2002, that she is not going to give up on the Defendant. But at the trial she stated she decided to leave him on the 23rd.

And guess what, 2 weeks later after the trial was over a juror came forward and stated that she bumped into the Defense Lawyer at the grocery store and stated to him that the baliff came into the jury room and told the jurors that they had to come up with a guilty verdict on something. They could not just let him go scott free. So the jurors found him guilty of intimidation, kidnapping, and sexually motivated specification.

And another witness stated that he seen the conspirator and the Defendant together after the allegations were supposed to have been made. He was called on the phone by the defense lawyer and the defense lawyer told him we will not need you because this seems to be a open and shut case.

A federal law officer stated to us,(the defendants family), that the documents they gave him would not make a difference in the case. This documents concerns what a juror stated about the defendants case.

He also stated that they were in a situation that they were going to have to twist the law a little. Also the signed statement from the juror was not and has not been given to the judge yet.

The federal officer stated they did not want this to go public. He also threatened us about not going public with the jurors statement that the baliff made them do. This statement was made in front of the Defendants Lawyer, his sister and other family members of the defendant.

The tape that we begged to be evidence in the trial the whole time the trial went on.

*Aug. 13@7:20am- I want to get f***ed so bad, I can just taste that d**k in my mouth. I can't believe this p***y is still wet. Call me back baby. Bye bye.*

*Aug. 13@7:23am- Hi, this is T***y again. I want to get f****d on my hands and knees while you pull my hair and call me b*****s and h**s when you f*****g me. When you get this message, call me back bye.*

*Aug.13@7:37am- Hey this is T***y ooh I want you so bad, I just want to stick my tongue in your a** so bad, I've been dreaming about you sucking on my t****s and my c***k, I just want to get f****d so bad, call me back baby.*

*Aug. 13@8:07am- Hey baby, I been waiting on you to call me, I'm over here craving that d**k of yours. So call me, I'm going to wait 5 or 10 minutes then I'm going to sleep.*

Aug.16@2:42pm- Hey this is T***y, you told me to leave you my fantasy, so my fantasy is to get f****d in your window while looking out of the window. Uh-Uh call me back later ah-ah.

Aug. @   - Hey baby, I was just thinking about my man this morning putting his big d**k in my mouth. It's so delicious to me. Do you have to work today; I'm going to try to make it up there early because I want to go for round 2. Call me back honey, bye bye.

Aug. 21@9:02am- Hey this T***y, you know we were meant to be you know I love you so much Please call me back. You said you be there for me, I'm just upset cause I'm going through some things. How could you leave somebody in their hour of need you said you be there. I'll never leave you in your hour of need. So like I said give me a call back, cause I'm never going to give up, I'm letting you know now bye.

Aug.22@8:20am-Yeah baby, I was just sitting back thinking about how I really and truly enjoy being with you, its like when we mad at each other, we try to be hard and all this and that. My heart is really with you and I really love you T***y and I just want to be with you forever, that's all I wanted to tell you. You have a nice day and you better not work too hard and you better be ready for me OK, bye.

Aug.24@12:33pm- You nasty a** no teeth, roach infested a** B**** you going to jail b****. Why in the f*** you think I was f*****g J-- for the last 5 years b****, he was over here earlier that's why I didn't want you over here, you nasty a** perverted a** b****, that's why you going to jail b**** thanks for your keys and the $25, you going to die b****. I'm going to get you h**, ah.

Aug.24@12:24pm- yes, you b**** you molesting little girls h**, me and S---- just had a long talk baby, I know all about you trying to get her to go to Alabama with you. You think I stop f*****g J---. My tubes are tied that's why I didn't get pregnant, you stupid a** b****. He got a pretty big d*** too. I never stop talking to J—, I tell him when to call. All the s**t is true baby about the dude in the white truck and the on in the red mustang, yeah I did go with D——. I know all about you, you nasty pervert, you wanted to be with a 12 year old girl and S——, she told me all about it. That's why you got to go to child support, you nasty a** perverted b****. That's why you going to die b****. R— and all of his gang are over here now, they looking for you b****. You going to h*** or jail. Leave town before Monday cause Monday you getting picked up.

Aug.24@10:47pm- Yeah b**** I heard you was f*****g a 15 year old girl when you and S— was together b****, you retarded a** h**. S— -told me she got Section 8 and you came over b**** and you was mad and her man J— was trying to get with her before you went to Alabama b****. You went through a big f******g deal cause it was 6 or 7 guys I was f*****g with b****. Come on Monday and you will be getting embarrassed on your job b****, I can't wait, I got a surprise for you. Go to work b****.

Aug.25@6:34am- B**** you better run to Birmingham h** cause come 7:00 Monday morning, the detective getting the statement b****. You go to work Monday, you going to get embarrassed h** trust me. The detective is coming for you h**, you going to jail h** like S---- said you was trying to get with her h**. You don't care about her having a baby as much as you talk about her like a dog. She know about everything you ever said.

The officer was told about the alleged incident, but he could not make a report on it because it was out of his jurisdiction.

This is the evidence that was never presented.

TITLE: Aggravated Menacing
DATE: 8-23-02.
INCIDENT REPORT: Conspirator cut the Defendants arm.

Victim reports that the suspect threatens to kill him. Victim stated the suspect came over with 3 friends with baseball bats stating they were going to kill him. Suspect continued to threaten him stating they were going to f**k him up and anyone that helped him, they also stated there could be some gunplay.

DESCRIPTION: Telephone Harassment
DATE REPORTED: 8-27-02.
DATE OCCURRED: 8-27-02.

ORIGINAL NARRATIVE:
  Victim states his ex-girlfriend continues to

call and harass him. She threatened to have him beat up. Victim has already been to the prosecutor and is being advised back to them.

DESCRIPTION: Child Endangering
DATE REPORTED: 11-15-01.
DATE OCCURRED: 11-13-01.

ORIGINAL NARRATIVE:
Reporting person states that between the dates above, the victim has been staying at the reporting person's home because the conspirator has not been willing to take the child back. Reporting person states that she attempted to contact the conspirator several times and was not able to contact her, so she contacted the CPD 542, who responded and info was received and JUV. was conveyed to residence where she lives. There was no response at the door. Reporting person stated that the conspirator told her she did not want the child at her home and would probably not answer the door. Victim was returned to reporting person's home, due to officers' belief

that the child would be safe and cared for, until her court date with child services on 11-16-01. Report titled endangering children due to guardian abandoning and neglecting victim (not reporting child missing several days at a time and guardians refusal to accept victim back into custodial care).

DESCRIPTION: Menacing-Telephone Harassment
DATE REPORTED: 2-11-00.
DATE OCCURRED: 2-11-00.

ORIGINAL NARRATIVE:
   Victim reports on above date N/S who is her ex-boyfriend, called her between 20-30 times and refused victim's request for N/S to stop calling.

DESCRIPTION: Assault
DATE REPORTED: 11-09-00.
DATE OCCURRED: 11-09-00.

ORIGINAL NARRATIVE:
   On the above date z/c 502 received a radio

broadcast to respond in connection with a female assaulted. Upon our arrival the victim stated the n.s. who had been drinking began a verbal argument with the victim. The N.S. then punched the victim in the face 2 or 3 times and then kicked the victim in the legs several times. The victim then left and called the police.

DESCRIPTION: Menacing and Telephone Harassment.
DATE REPORTED: 5-28-01.
DATE OCCURRED: 5-28-01.

ORIGINAL NARRATIVE:

Victim states she broke up with NS on 5-27-01. He came over today at approx. 4:30pm, went over by her car which was parked in the driveway. Victim states that she believed NS was going to do damage to her, also became violent as he had in the past, so the victim went out to talk to him. Victim states NS became irritated and aggressive and started to approach her in a threatening manner. Victim states that she believed he was going to hit her, so to prevent from being hit, she grabbed his arm. Victim states that NS twisted her arm and began to threaten her and her son, saying that he was going to jump on him. She believes NS would do this because of his abusive nature in the past.

DESCRIPTION: Assault
DATE REPORTED: 5-19-01.
DATE OCCURRED: 5-19-01.

ORIGINAL NARRATIVE:
   Victim states offender assaulted her. Victim states offender was visiting her and they began arguing because he wanted her old license plates. Victim states offender got angry and hit her on the left side of her face. No visible injury, EMS refused.

This is evidence that shows how devious the conspirator really is.

DESCRIPTION: Telephone Harassment
DATE REPORTED: 8-30-01.
DATE OCCURRED: 8-14-01.

ORIGINAL NARRATIVE:

Victim states NS started calling victim since 8-14-01 at approx. 9:30am and NS calls victim at different times a day approx. 3 times in the am and 3 times in pm, making threats that NS will get someone to jump on the victim and will get victims children taken from victim. Victim states NS is victims natural sister and was having problems since their father passed away.

Several weeks later after the incident was reported the conspirators sister was admitted in the hospital because she was very ill and she wanted her to come to see her in the hospital because she knew she was on her death bed, but she refused to go see her and she died.

After hearing all the evidence that we presented to the judge after the defendant was found guilty of the charges, the judge made him sign a document while he was incarcerated for 6 months. He would take probation then she took herself off the case and assigned it to another judge so that the new judge can give the defendant probation from the document she made him sign to take probation.

You are in debt from the day you were born. The day you were born, your insurance does not cover medical costs from when you have a baby. The WIC they give you is not enough to keep milk in the house for the baby. You have all of these holidays that seem to come every other month, and in the process of trying to pay all the bills, rent, and insurance; you have many distractions. Some other distractions include: Taking your children to school and daycare and then going to all of these meetings they have you going to, talking about your child's behavior, and you already know about your child. While you are going shopping for x-mas, you get stuck in traffic and you spend all of your money and then you're back in debt again. And if you are not living with your children and children's mother is on welfare or if she has a job that pays her money than you make, they take most of your money out of your income tax. But with your income tax check: that is how you try to get out of debt from x-mas, but they want to take it for child support. If you got a college grant they take it from your income tax check also. So why does the day that is suppose to be the best day of the year, just make you wish it would be all over and done with? So when you decide to settle down, you and your family will be in debt for the rest of your lives. And you can't file your kids on your income tax claim if the mother does, except for every 3 years. You will be so in debt, you will die owing the state money.

"Santa Clause is coming to town..." goes the lyrics of a song we have all heard. "You'd better watch out..." are also the lyrics of the same song. The latter is a warning to the wise. Why?
HISTORY, which is best qualified to reward all research, tells us many things not taught today. The science of etymology, a science most African-Americans know least about, informs us of the authentic meaning of words, names, etc. Etymology and History gives us a lucid insight into "Santa Clause."
"Santa Clause" nickname is "St Nick" which means, according to Webster's research... "The devil." Note the prefix "St." in the "nick"-

name. Devil - a saint...? "Santa Clause"- the

devil...? We all should peruse the matter.

When mental acumen is employed, one can clearly see the devil the name "Santa." What happens when the "n" is moved from the middle of the word and placed at the end of it...? What word or name do you find? Webster states that "Santa Clause" is a "corrupted name." The name "Saint Nicholas," according to Webster, is not a positive appellative. "Santa Clause" and "Satan" are one. The Bible (2-Corin. 11:14,15) states that "Satan is transformed into an angel of light" - that's Santa.

SANTA CLAUSE has and employs "reindeer" to visit the homes of human beings. He has a bag full of "toys." What are toys? Toys are tools of trash. What are tools used for...?

What is "rein-deer?" The word "rein" is from the Latin word "retinere" - which means: "to hold back." Reins are used by a rider to govern a horse or other animal. The word rein also means, according to Webster, "a curbing"; "a check"; "hindrance"; "position of command..."; "to direct"; "guide"; "control."

The term – "to give free rein to" means to "give free play to" ...i.e. the imagination. "Reins" means also... "the seat of the feelings or passions.: The word "deer," in its root meaning, means "beast"; "wild animal."

When "rein" and "deer" are concatenated, a beast or wild animal that directed or guided or free, comes into reality. If a beast or wild animal is directed or guided there is much to consider under the caption of positiveness... and negativeness. Some wild animals are guided and directed to do evil or harm to people. So the question is... "Guided or directed by whom and to do what?" There isn't much good a beast or wild animal can do... even when guided.

It is lucid that if a wild animal is rendered free rein or let loose to move about without any control..."you'd better watch out...." Be careful.

Santa Clause is Satan. How would Satan use a beast or wild animal? How would Satan use the "seat of the feeling or passion" (the heart)? For good or evil? The Bible (Gen. 3:1) states that Satan is the most subtle of all *beasts.*

WHEN THE NAMES of Santa's, or Satan's, reindeer are analyzed, we find hidden direction for the masses. Insidious desires are quickened.

The Quran directs the wise to reflect and to ponder. Reflect means to "look again." Ponder means to "weigh in the mind" or "carefully check out a thing so nothing important escapes attention." Shall we...? Let's.

ONE OF THE reindeer is named "Dancer." What does "Dancer" means? It means "to perform, to a rhythmic and patterned succession of movements, commonly to music." Dancer is "dance" actualized. Look into society, do we see this "reindeer?" What type of music are such deer dancing to? Who authored the notes (a note is a message)? Is it not music designed to allow or direct the "animal nature" in low-minded people to run wild or free?

Listen to some of the titles of the songs people dance(r) to... "Freak-Out!"; "I Want To Do Something Freakish To You"; "Get Down

On It"; "Shake Your Booty"; "Cold Blooded"; "Help Yourself To My Love"; "Nasty Girl"; etc.

Look at the word "Disco." In it we find the name of the Roman god of the Underworld - "Dis." A record is a "Dis(c)." "Dis" is a prefix meaning: "deprive of"; "cease"; "fail"; etc.

The first part of the appellative "Dancer" is "dan." The Bible (Gen. 49:17) states that "dan" deported himself like Satan. Dan biteth the "heel" of amount of the rider and induces the "rider" to "fall backward." Dan is an "adder in the path" of the human being. Dan is a snakish demeanor in people.

The Quran (7:10-17) states that Iblis promised the Creator that he would lie in wait for the human being. Iblis said he would lie in the path of the human being and influence said from the left, right, before and behind. Such is the case.

Dancer is Dan active in society. The heel or lowest part of the person, the animal Naf, causes the intelligence to fall backward (not forward). The Quran (25:43) covers this.

"Comet" is another reindeer driven by Santa

Clause(Satan). In its etymology it means... "longhaired." Webster states that it means... an irregular body in form, that's luminous, and follows an orbit..." This is also a trend in society today. But note what the Bible (I Corin.11:14) says about it. Look at the shame in this society. Hair also has a spiritual/intellectual meaning - it's esoteric or symbolic.

"Cupid," another reindeer; this is the name of the Roman god of "erotic love." Being strongly affected by "sexual Desire." Look at all the rape and lewdness in society. Today the words "love" and "sex" and "sleep" and "bed" are synonymous.

"Dasher," another reindeer. This means "to affect by mixing in something different." The Bible (St. Matt. 16:6-12) states ... "beware of the leaven of the Pharisees and of the Saducees"...i.e. their doctrine. bread in scripture means religious teaching.

"Prancer," another reindeer; this means... "sublimely pleased with oneself." A prancer is a show-off. Pretentious. This trend is debilitating the African-American. When one is pleased with self, such one doesn't see the need for self-improvement.

"Donner," another reindeer. To don means "to envelop oneself in." Another trend in society. People have become thoroughly involved in wrong doing. Let it all hang out...do your own thing. Self-destruct.

"Blitzen," another reindeer. What is a blitz? Webster states... " a rush of the passer by the defensive linebackers..." This trend is seen in the frequent bombardment of the minds with concepts which cause the masses to respond more easily to corruption. The Bible alludes to this reality (2 Peter 2:1-3; 1Peter 5:8; Colossians 2:8).

"Vixen," another reindeer; Vixen is a shrewd female of loose morals. Vixen also means an ill-tempered woman. Woman in scriptural language means society. None can negate the fact that this society of America is one loose and ill morals!

"Rudolph," another reindeer. The leader of them all. **"Rudolph the Red Nosed Reindeer."** There is a special song about this reindeer. There is also a song about the "little Red

Caboose behind the train." Red Nose and **Red Caboose** - one up front and one behind...

IS THERE A connection? Remember the promise of Iblis...? "Red" represents passion. One of the meanings of "rein" is the seat of passions or feelings." Rudolph means "reddish." Here is a reindeer with a name that means "red" and, with a red nose. When one's "nose is open," it means "passions" are affected or "feelings" are open to influences. The nose of society at large is wide open to Satan's influences. Satan is Santa and is the driver of the evil trends at large in society.

The Santa Clause story in scripture is lucid to the wise (Hosea 4:6-14). The Reindeer all represent social trends (Jer. 5-26-28). The merchants are pointed out clearly. They surely wax fat off dollars and cents of the gullible masses. A red nose and (Satan) a red body.

Is all this coincidental?

Santa Clause enters the homes via chimneys. The word "chimney" means furnace or "fireplace." Fire is "red" and "hot" and Satan's said familiar residence. Santa is fat (Philippians 3:19)... He is a pig - this same *attitude and appetite is common in society.*

The Quran says that obesity is a sin. Santa/Satan is sinful. "...You'd better watch out... Santa Clause is coming to town...He knows when you are sleeping...He knows when you are awake." So? "So be good for goodness sake." (Holy Quran 39:35-41).

Something I have done to see where my family and the Americans hearts are, on Voting.

Change Our World
"Vote"
Power to the Parents
Future for the Children

We are urging you to VOTE. There are many reasons why it is important for you to vote. Amongst those reasons are the simple liberties that we deserve. For instance there are laws that regulate how you discipline your children. Is this fair? If you don't vote you are allowing someone else to tell you how to raise your children. I feel there should be some laws in place to this affect because some people do go overboard and abuse their children. However, some parents know how to discipline their children properly. These are the parents that pay along with the bad apples. This should be a topic that we can vote on along with other issues of importance to us. Such as children killing children. Our children have a difficult challenge ahead of them. They must see a bright future in a world that does not show them one. We need to participate in electing the officials that will decide their future. Someone who cares about the children not just themselves or how many votes they can get. Another issue that affects us directly is Welfare rights. Many people were thrown off welfare and sent to mediocre schools for training that they can not find a job to use. Some of these people had felonies and really can't find a place of employment because of that. This is why we are sponsoring a VOTERS REGISTRATION DRIVE. There are many locations to follow. Transportation will be provided to and from these locations only to register to vote and on Election Day to vote. We are encouraging you to vote so that the turnout will be greater this year. Maybe we can get some officials in office that will think about our future and the futures of our children.

We shall never forget those that fought for our right to VOTE!

Susan B. Anthony
Martin Luther King Jr.
Malcolm X
Medgar Evers
JFK (proved voting does make a difference)

PETITION

We are urging you to VOTE for many reasons. It is imperative that you be able to assist in making decisions concerning your everyday life. Are you comfortable with others telling you how, why, and when to discipline your children? Is this fair? There are parents who know how to discipline their children properly, just as there are those who hack good parenting skills and go overboard. Why should all of those parents suffer the same? Discipline in homes should be a topic that we can VOTE on along with other issues of importance in our community. Children are killing children. Can we afford to leave the lives of our children in the hands of those who may not even have their best interest in heart? Our children have a difficult challenge ahead of them. It is our responsibility to ensure that they see a bright future in a world that does not show them one. We have a duty to elect officials that will decide their futures. We need someone who cares more about our children than themselves or the number of votes they can attain.

PETITION

We are urging you to sign this PETITION on the issue of WELFARE RIGHTS. It affects us directly in many different ways. Hundreds of people were removed from the Welfare System and sent to mediocre schools for training that was proved useless in the job world. Some are not even able to find jobs because they are convicted felons, regardless of the amount of education they have. Also, why is the government paying more money to other people for watching your children than they give you a month when you are on Welfare?

Example: They give the Daycare Provider $400 a week just for caring for 1 child for a few hours, when they give you $550 a month for 4 children; how is that fair?

By signing this PETITION, you can help others and also help yourselves.

POLITICALLY DAMNED PROBLEMS OF THE WORLD

TO WHOM IT MAY CONCERN:

I, Derrick Brown wrote this book on all the problems the politicians caused from their decisions that they made. If you have any problems or issues about the decisions the politicians have made, send them to Politically Damn@aol.com

Thank You

Servants of God for the Strengthen of Families

May 23, 20

Neighborhood Outreach
8515 Madison Ave.
Cleveland, Ohio 44102
(216) 281-5081 - Fax (216) 281-5085

Dear Friends of the community,
Today's community is one of our greatest investments. It's the key to creating a better lifestyle in our community and us. Our positive self awareness will promote determination for different cultures in our community. June 2001 Neighborhood Outreach helped 75 families with housing and our food pantry has helped over 150 families with emergency food. We've helped children of the community with shoes and clothes when in need.

During the holiday seasons we help with the baskets for over 200 families with the need of our help. We our recognized by Mayor Jane Cambell, Councilman Westbrook, and many other agency throughout the city of Cleveland. Neighborhood Outreach is a 5013C nonprofit Community Service Organization whose mission is to improve the quality of life within our communities. In continuing our efforts to provide these services and many more we need your financial support.

Our Outreach center would like to promote community affairs and literacy programs, your donations are tax-deduction. Your contributions can help us continue to carry our mission. It will only take a moment to make a heartfelt decision to support Neighborhood Outreach. Please help us with the need of our community.

Thank You for your generosity

God Bless
Mr. and Mrs. Jappie Pulley
C.E.O. & Executive Director

1ˢᵗ letter received from someone who wishes the world would change.

The story of America's prison system surrounding the war on drugs.

White Supremacy is at the core of every situation surrounding the so-called war on drugs. (BLACK PEOPLE)

The war on drugs are now tied to legitimate corporate profits. Prisons are a growth industry. They use prison labor to amass private wealth.

Our present prison systems can be considered a 2000's version of American Slavery. There is a business incentive to sustain drug crime in our society. It is a disgrace that our people sit by idle while millions of people are enslaved under the guise of a war on drugs and tough on crime policies.

We have to remember the 13ᵗʰ Amendment to the constitution did not abolish slavery in 1865. The Amendment read's "Neither slavery nor involuntary servitude, except as punishment for a crime where of the party shall have been duly convicted shall exist within the United States, or any place subject to their jurisdiction."

Slavery is live and back in these prisons, all over America. Federal and State Government produce an economic benefit by building prisons.

We must keep our black politicians focused on the racism target in order to gain full freedom, justice, and equality within future generations.

Get up black men and women and stand up in the fight against the so-called drug laws! Genocide is surely in effect if you only understood.

The New world order and Dawning of a New day For communism and The Republic of America!

POLITICALLY DAMNED

Problems Of The World

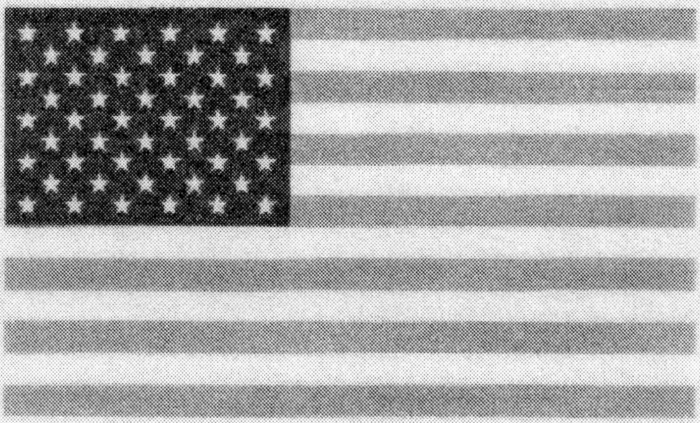